WADSWORTH PHILO

ON
ROUSSEAU

Sally Scholz
Villanova University

Australia • Canada • Mexico • Singapore • Spain
United Kingdom • United States

COPYRIGHT © 2001 Wadsworth, a division of Thomson Learning, Inc. Thomson Learning™ is a trademark used herein under license.

ALL RIGHTS RESERVED. No part of this work covered by the copyright hereon may be reproduced or used in any form or by any means—graphic, electronic, or mechanical, including photocopying, recording, taping, Web distribution, or information storage and retrieval systems—without the written permission of the publisher.

Printed in the United States of America
2 3 4 5 6 7 04 03 02 01

For permission to use material from this text, contact us:
Web: http://www.thomsonrights.com
Fax: 1-800-730-2215
Phone: 1-800-730-2214

For more information, contact:
Wadsworth/Thomson Learning, Inc.
10 Davis Drive
Belmont, CA 94002-3098
USA
http://www.wadsworth.com

ISBN: 0-534-58368-7

Table of Contents

Chapter 1　　Introduction 1
Chapter 2　　Biography 7
Chapter 3　　Education 28
Chapter 4　　Politics 63
Chapter 5　　Arts and Letters 80
Bibliography 91

1
Introduction

Among the most quoted lines in philosophy is Jean-Jacques Rousseau's "Man was born free, and everywhere he is in chains." This sentence from the first book of the *Social Contract* contains the key to understanding the life and work of Rousseau as well as the tremendous impact he left on art, politics, and society.

Jean-Jacques Rousseau, 1712-1778, argued that individuals were by nature good but that society corrupted them through its false pretenses. In essence, society replaced morality with propriety, and truth and virtue with useless knowledge and idleness. We are "born free" and good but enslave ourselves, "in chains," with public opinion. A well governed society, however, might allow individuals to continue in their natural goodness. Rousseau wrote essays, treatises, literature, and letters to try to convey his system of thought but he also recognized that very few people would have the gifts of nature that would allow them to understand his thought. To appreciate his work, Rousseau believed the reader needed sentiment as well as reason, virtue and a passion for the truth as well as natural instincts.

In his day, Rousseau's work was both glorified and vilified. He began his career as a philosopher with an essay contest in 1749 at the age of 37. This essay contest marked not only the start of a brilliant career, it also opened the floodgates for Rousseau's articulation of a system that would eventually transform Europe. In the rest of this introduction, three main elements of Rousseau's system are presented in brief. These three also indicate some of the most important areas of influence left by

Introduction

Rousseau's work. Subsequent chapters further explain these elements in relation to Rousseau's autobiography, his work on education, his political theory, and his contributions to artistic and literary study.

Man of nature v. man of society

Rousseau was born at a transition period in thought and politics. Many have debated whether he is best understood as representing the classic thought of the ancients such as Plato and Aristotle or the modern thought of the likes of Hobbes and Locke. Both interpretations are probably correct. Like the ancients, Rousseau defended virtue; like the moderns, he defended the individual. Rousseau is of the Age of Enlightenment and one of its greatest critics. He is often counted among the *philosophes* with Diderot and Voltaire and yet he argued against their projects to disseminate knowledge widely. In some ways, Rousseau embodies all the contradictions of his time.

Another remarkable feature of the time period in which Rousseau was born is the rise of the city. Whereas previous generations had lived scattered across the countryside, Rousseau's contemporaries rushed to the city to find fame and fortune. These crowded urban areas created their own standards of morality according to the fickle winds of fashion. Certainly physical disease spread and Rousseau would be quick to add that moral depravity grew as well.

Within this context, Rousseau began to explain his system of thought. He wanted to restore individual humans to their natural goodness through educational and political reforms. A well-governed society, he said, would preserve natural goodness. His educational reforms focused on creating the man of nature through a careful use of experience rather than books or lectures. His political reforms used the social contract to advance the general will thereby upholding the goodness of individuals by making that the goodness of the state as well.

But who is this man of nature so vaunted by Rousseau? And what is so wicked about the man of society? Rousseau's novel, discussed in the fifth chapter of this book, illustrates the difference between the man of nature and the man of society. One of the main characters, St. Preux, is in love with the daughter of nobility. In an effort to win her father over to his side, he is described as the man of nature although he does not have social standing.

> All the gifts that cannot be acquired by men, he has received from nature, and he has added to them all the talents he could acquire on his own. He is young, tall, handsome, robust, clever; he has education, good sense, morals, courage; he has a polished mind, a sound soul ... In a word, if you prefer reason to prejudice, and if you love your daughter better than your titles, it is to him you will give her. (*Julie*, 138)

The man of nature, as evidenced by St. Preux and Emile in Rousseau's treatise on education, is the man who uses the gifts nature has given him and develops them into the true morality. We start as isolated individuals naturally free and naturally good. Nature gives us two instincts that develop into morality: self-preservation and pity. Self-preservation or love of self guides us in the state of nature. There is no morality because that implies social intercourse. Pity is the natural sentiment felt when we witness the suffering of others. If these two are carefully developed or nurtured, then when the individual is ready for social intercourse he or she will follow virtue rather than public opinion. Rousseau also took care to show how, when he reached the proper age, the man of nature developed his sentiments and, combined with reason, became moral. This development is explain in *Emile* and summarized in Chapter 3.

Rousseau disdained the prejudices of society or social opinions and conventions. These merely obscure the man of nature and replace virtue with propriety. They also reveal inequality but this inequality is not a natural inequality. On the contrary, Rousseau contends that inequality arises because of property; social conventions legalize that inequality.

In short, the man of nature is the individual in his or her natural goodness caring only for virtue. The man of society subjects himself to social conventions and sacrifices virtue to public opinion.

Father of Romanticism

As is evident from the above, Rousseau eschewed social conventions in favor of nature. He also valued emotion although not to the expense of reason. Whereas in the past humans were viewed in opposition to nature, Rousseau aimed at uniting man and nature. This is one reason many call Rousseau the father of Romanticism. Romanticism was an intellectual and artistic movement in 18th and 19th century Europe contrasting with

Introduction

Classicism. Classicism was more interested in accurate imitation inspired by antiquity with an emphasis on form and simplicity. The art of Ancient Greece and Rome were the standards or ideals. In contrast, Romanticism valued individual expression, emotion, and nature. Romanticism also sought to identify the hero or beautiful soul.

Rousseau's *Confessions* for example are a good example of the Romantic movement. In his autobiography, Rousseau tried to present an honest picture of his faults as well as his strengths rather than make his life story a testament to the Creator. This looking into the self helped to set a standard for Romanticism both in its emphasis on the personal and its search for explanations in childhood for adult character traits.

In both *Emile* and *Julie,* Rousseau professes a faith contrary to both the atheism of many of his contemporary *philosophes* and the dogmatism of the Catholic Church. This demonstrates some of Rousseau's opposition to Enlightenment rationalism, another characteristic of the Romantic movement. This opposition is also evidenced in his writings on the arts and sciences.

In art, Rousseau sought simplicity though rarely the simplicity of Classicism. Instead, his proposal for artistic amusement in Geneva consisted of the cultural dances of the people. These dances and the hard work within the community that made the recreational activities so enjoyable illustrate Rousseau's argument that happiness never strays far from nature. As we see in Chapter 3, Rousseau's education is designed to foster the gifts of nature and thus make Emile, his imaginary student, truly content.

In epistemology, Rousseau also foreshadowed the Romantic movement with his preferences of experience over intellect. In contrast to his friends among the *philosophes*, contrary to increasing the access to the arts and sciences, Rousseau argued that the Enlightenment proliferation of knowledge only encouraged humans in their wickedness. Study of useless information for the sake of public opinion made individuals idle and weak. Rousseau would rather have humans exercise the body and allow the mind to develop as part of this exercise. For example, as we farm the land we learn of growth patterns, natural pesticides, weather, geography, soil conditions, and countless other useful bits of knowledge. Reading about these things in books merely lets the body grow limp from being sedentary.

Rousseau helped to bring about one of the major intellectual and artistic transitions in Western history; more detail of his position regarding the Arts and Letters may be found in Chapter 5. But

Rousseau's romantic ideals were not without political ramifications. Rousseau occasionally calls for a revolution in his writings – a revolution that would liberate the poor and oppressed. Although it is doubtful that he had the French Revolution in mind, his ideas inspired key actors of that revolution.

Philosopher of the French Revolution

In *Reveries of a Solitary Walker* Rousseau tells the reader about his favorite island, Island of Saint-Pierre in the middle of the Lake of Bienne. After explaining some of the geography and erosion patterns (a smaller island losing its land mass as the waves transfer it to the larger island), he makes a telling statement about his political and economic position: "Thus it is that the substance of the poor always goes to enrich the wealthy" (Reveries, 82). Rousseau wrote about the extreme disparity between the rich and the poor. The rich were respected for no reason other than their wealth while the poor were treated cruelly. When a rich man is injured, all rush to his aid but when a poor man is injured, no one helps him because he cannot pay. In addition, Rousseau was critical of magistrates who ruled arbitrarily and often favored the wealthy classes in their legislation. His political writings emphasized liberty and equality making Rousseau a champion of democracy. However, his politics, which include state run censorship, have also been criticized for being totalitarian.

Rousseau saw his political theory as an extension of the man of nature. His *Social Contract* was an attempt to create social compacts that allowed truth and virtue to flourish in society rather than become obscured by meaningless conventions. His state is tightly regulated but the regulation is according to the will of the people themselves. Such things as censorship are used to encourage humans in their goodness. Thus Rousseau argues that at times humans must be forced to be free.

Perhaps the two most influential ideas on the French Revolution are his rejection of the arbitrary rule of the monarchy and his hatred of inequality that results originally from property and then becomes cemented in social mores and laws. A monarchy itself arises only because of a great disparity in wealth between the classes. Rousseau argued that the people ought to always be Sovereign and their will, the general will, was always directed toward the common good.

Introduction

While he probably would not have approved of the violent tactics of the Reign of Terror during the French Revolution, Rousseau certainly laid the foundation for it with his radical ideas of the people's power. Chapter 4 develops these political ideas further.

Troubled Genius

Jean-Jacques Rousseau was, without question, a brilliant philosopher. He was inspired by Montaigne, Montesquieu, Plutarch, Locke, and Plato among others. He inspired Immanuel Kant, Karl Marx, John Dewey, Simone de Beauvoir and countless others. But he was also an incredibly troubled genius. He died in relative obscurity after having been exiled from France. He had been attacked in the press for his radical ideas regarding the Church and politics. His house had been stoned, and in his own thoughts, he had been rejected by his former friends for the lifestyle he adopted. In the end, Rousseau felt he had remained faithful to his ideals to live simply and to love truth:

> Holy and pure truth to whom I have consecrated my life, never will my passions soil the sincere love which I have for thee; neither interest nor fear can corrupt the homage that I am wont to offer to thee, and my pen will refuse thee only what it fears to accord to vengeance. (*Letter to D'Alembert*, 132f)

Rousseau thought that his former friends were conniving against him because what he had to say was so dangerous. The truth, so contrary to social conventions and so simple, was also quite hated. But as Rousseau himself taught us in his *Confessions*, it is often instructive to look at the entire life in order to understand the man and his thought.

2
Biography

Jean-Jacques Rousseau's *Confessions* set a new standard for autobiographical writing. Autobiography no longer needed to be an expression of religious experience for the benefit of others. Together with *Reveries of a Solitary Walker* and *Rousseau, Judge of Jean-Jacques* (often called *Dialogues*), the *Confessions* offer a picture of Rousseau's life through his own eyes as well as a glimpse into the troubled personality of this brilliant man. Examples of paranoia abound in the second part of the *Confessions*; indeed, he was convinced that many great thinkers and socialites were conspiring together against him. He believed that his decision to live according to his principles – to try to become the man of Nature – was sufficiently threatening as to provoke the ire of his friends and colleagues. He wrote the *Confessions* both as a defense of his life and as a simply explanation of his life. Rousseau completed the book in 1770; it was published in 1781, three years after his death. Rousseau describes his aim in the opening remarks:

> I have displayed myself as I was, as vile and despicable when my behaviour was such, as good, generous, and noble when I was so. I have bared my secret soul as Thou thyself hast seen it, Eternal Being! So let the numberless legion of my fellow men gather round me, and hear my confessions. Let them groan at my depravities, and blush for my misdeed. But let each one of them reveal his heart at the foot of Thy throne with equal sincerity, and may any man who dares, say "I was a better man than he." (*Confessions*, 17)

Biography

With this explanation, Jean-Jacques Rousseau begins the story of his life with the story of his birth in Geneva on June 28, 1712 to Isaac Rousseau and Susanne Bernard. His father was a watchmaker and his mother was the daughter of a minister. They had one other son, seven years older than Rousseau. This brother ran away and disappeared. He is mentioned a few times in passing in the *Confessions* but never by name. Rousseau proudly wore the title of Citizen of Geneva. Male Citizens twenty years old or older, as opposed to Subjects, Inhabitants, and Natives, were privileged to vote.

Rousseau's mother Susanne died in childbirth leaving his father Isaac grief stricken. Rousseau calls his birth the first of his misfortunes. Reflecting on this incident, Rousseau says, "I felt before I thought" (*Confessions*, 19). This reverses the order Rousseau would have his own pupil develop according to his treatise on education, *Emile*. Feeling ought to follow reasoning and be subject to it. Rousseau is very critical of the education system of his time. He faults it primarily for creating weak, dependent individuals who enslave themselves to social opinion. Education has the power to obscure or enhance the gifts of nature.

When Jean-Jacques was merely 10 years old his father was forced to leave Geneva. Rousseau claims his father left on principle but the latter had fought with a member of Council and, while Rousseau implies that his father may have punched the Council member, history says he wounded Pierre Gautier with a sword. Perceiving he was not being treated fairly, Rousseau says his father "preferred to leave Geneva and remain abroad for the rest of his life rather than lose both liberty and honour by giving in" (*Confessions*, 23). Isaac did not bring his son to Lyon with him but left him in the care of Rousseau's uncle Bernard who had a son close to Rousseau's age. These two were sent to live with M. Lambercier, a Protestant pastor who undertook their education.

The two cousins stayed at M. Lambercier's for two years, a period which Rousseau describes with evident contentment primarily because of the country living. Rousseau relates an amusing story regarding a small willow tree. M. Lambercier had planted a walnut tree to provide shade to a terrace. Rousseau and his cousin planted a young willow near-by without the permission of M. Lambercier. Since the tree needed water and since the children were not allowed to get the water, they cleverly built "an aquaduct" from the walnut tree to their willow tree. M. Lambercier discovered it and tore it up but did not punish the cousins. Instead, Rousseau reports hearing him laugh heartily from his sister's room shortly after the incident.

This relationship with M. Lambercier and his sister soured when Rousseau was falsely accused of breaking the teeth of Mlle Lambercier's combs as they sat on the stove. Being so falsely accused marked the end of "the serenity of [his] childish life" (*Confessions*, 30). Although the cousins stayed a bit longer with M. Lambercier, they did not enjoy it and soon Rousseau's uncle took them away.

Rousseau also recalls the development of his sexual tastes and the emergence of his desires. He discovered sensuality while being punished by Mlle Lambercier for some minor disobedience. Shortly thereafter, Mlle Lambercier gave up the practice of beating Rousseau and also expelled him and his cousin from her room where they had slept (in winter they slept in her bed). Rousseau was now considered a big boy. No doubt Mlle Lambercier had seen signs of his sensual delight in being punished by her. He often repeats his desire for a dominating lover in the *Confessions* and his romanticized ideal of love describes women as forcing men into submissions by controlling their hearts. Rousseau describes his own desire as such a submission to his beloved: "To fall on my knees before a masterful mistress, to obey her commands, to have to beg for her forgiveness, have been to me the most delicate of pleasures; and the more my vivid imagination heated my blood the more like a spellbound lover I looked" (*Confessions*, 28).

As his father was still in Lyon, it was up to his Uncle Bernard to decide where Rousseau would next seek education. After an unsuccessful apprenticeship with the City Registrar, Rousseau was apprenticed to an engraver for five years. Rousseau describes his life up to this point as a life of "simple liberty." Under the master however, he became restrained and fearful. He grew to envy the liberty of the master and journeyman and covet all that was deprived to him. This reflection echoes Rousseau's claim in *Emile, Second Discourse,* and *Social Contract* that "Unsatisfied desires always lead to...vice" (*Confessions*, 41). Equality of possession is required, otherwise inequality inspires vice. Rousseau began to steal what he desired. Although he was beaten for his transgressions, he soon came to see the punishment as simply an exchange; rather than discouraging him from stealing, the beatings authorized him to continue. As he says, "I reckoned that to be beaten like a rogue justified my being one" (*Confessions*, 43). This experience reveals what Rousseau calls the principle facet of his character: he is a man of passion.

> My passions are extremely strong, and while I am under their sway nothing can equal my impetuosity. I am amenable to no restraint,

> respect, fear, or decorum. I am cynical, bold, violent, and daring. No shame can stop me, no fear of danger alarm me. Except for the one object in my mind the universe for me is non-existent. But all this lasts only a moment; and the next moment plunges me into complete annihilation. Catch me in a calm mood, I am all indolence and timidity. Everything alarms me, everything discourages me. I am frightened by a buzzing fly. I am too lazy to speak a word or make a gesture. So much am I a slave to fears and shames that I long to vanish from mortal sight. (*Confessions*, 44)

But perhaps more telling for his philosophy, this story divulges a central component of Rousseau's thought: desire leads to servitude. So long as our needs are simple and what we want is within our reach, we are happy. But when our desires exceed the simple provisions that nature provides, and when these desires become needs, we are thrown into misery. Human beings, then, are the source of their own suffering.

Rousseau left Geneva at the age of 16. His decision to leave was more by accident than anything else. He resolved not to return after arriving too late at the gate. Two previous occasions he was locked outside the city gates – he and his friends had merely gone out to enjoy some games – and his master (only 7 years older than Rousseau) punished him severely each time, promising a much more severe punishment if he was locked out a third time. When the third occasion presented itself, he simply resolved not to return to the city at all. Noting the way equality of birth gave way to inequality of social position, Rousseau asked that his cousin come to the gate to say goodbye. They had grown apart because Rousseau was a poor apprentice while his cousin Bernard was "a lad of the upper town." At the tender age of 16, the young man who would become the philosopher of equality embarked on a new stage of life characterized by travel and conversion to Catholicism. Rousseau met his new fate with apprehension and delight:

> Terrible though the moment had appeared in which fear prompted me to fly, when the time came to carry out my plan I found it quite delightful. Although no more than a child, to leave my country and my relations and everyone who might sustain or support me; to throw up an apprenticeship half completed without knowing my trade well enough to live by it; to incur the miseries of poverty without any means of ending them; in the weakness and innocence of my youth to expose myself to all the temptations of vice and

despair; to court evils, errors, traps, slavery, and death in a distant land, beneath a far less merciful yoke than the one I had just found intolerable: that was what I was about to do, that was the perspective which I should have envisaged. How different was the future I imagined! The only thought in my mind was the independence I believed I had won. Now that I was free and my own master, I supposed that I could do anything, achieve anything. I had only to take one leap, and I could rise and fly through the air. I marched confidently out into the world's wide spaces. Soon they would be filled with my fame. Everywhere I went I should find feastings, treasures, and adventures, friends ready to help me and mistresses eager to do my pleasure. The moment I showed myself the universe would be busy with my concerns. Not the whole universe, however. I could to some extent do without that; I did not require so much. One charming circle would be enough; more would be an embarrassment. Modestly I imagined myself one of a narrow but exquisitely chosen clan, over which I felt confident that I should rule. A single castle was the limit of my ambition. To be the favourite of its lord and lady, the lover of their daughter, the friend of their son, and protector of their neighbours: that would be enough; I required no more. (*Confessions*, 52)

Rousseau went to Confignon in Savoy a mere 16 miles from Geneva. There he met a priest, M. de Pontverre, who saw in Rousseau a possible convert to Catholicism. This priest sent Rousseau to Annecy to see Mme de Warens. Mme de Warens was a 29 year old recent convert to Catholicism who was given a pension of two thousand francs by the King of Sardinia. The priests compelled her to share this pension with wanderers they sent to her in the hopes of winning converts. Rousseau's meeting with Louise Éléonore de Warens would changed his life but at this point she packed him off to Turin to study Catholicism. Rousseau describes the monastery's inhabitants as riff-raff, ruffians even, who joined him in exchanging faith for a meal.

Describing this experience gave Rousseau pause to reflect on sin in his *Confessions*. Sin, he says, results not from our weakness which might ultimately be credited to God as our creator thereby making God the author of our sin; instead sin results from our human failures to act according to God's will. Rousseau uses the analogy of an abyss to further explain: "So finally, as we tumble into the abyss, we ask God why he has made us so feeble. But, in spite of ourselves, He replies through our consciences: 'I have made you too feeble to climb out of the pit, because I made you strong enough not to fall in'" (*Confessions*, 69).

Upon leaving the monastery, Rousseau boarded with a Mme Basile who eventually arranged for him to work. For a short time, he was the valet of the Countess de Vercellis. Her health was failing and as death approached people's thoughts turned to her fortune. She had no children and her nephew was set to inherit but she would also remember kindly all of her devoted attendants. These attendants, as Rousseau tells the story, recognized that he was not in his right place and feared that their mistress might use part of her fortune to put him there. Naturally, this would diminish their take. Although he had been quite attentive previously, these other servants conspired to keep Rousseau out of her sight to such an extent that when she wrote her will she had not seen him in over a week. He was left completely out of the will.

As the estate was being distributed, a pink and silver ribbon belonging to the niece (Mlle Pontal) of the chief servants (M. and Mme Lorenzi) disappeared. Rousseau stole it and when he was found with it he claimed he got it from a servant named Marion. She was the cook and was considered very trustworthy, though according to Rousseau she was not very pretty. The other servants and the Countess's nephew were shocked to hear her name. She defended herself and asked Rousseau not to disgrace himself with a lie but he held firm in his accusation. They were both dismissed. This lie marked Rousseau for life. He often referred back to it and attributes his "loathing of untruth" to this single lie. True to predictions, his conscience punished him more than any other punishment could have. Rousseau admits being afraid of disgrace but not punishment (*Confessions*, 88).

Rousseau was beginning to meet new people and among them was a Savoyard vicar by the name of M. Gaime. He, together with a M. Gâtier whom Rousseau would meet later at a seminary Mme de Warens sent him to, form the model for the "Confessions of a Savoyard Vicar" in the *Emile*.

At the initiation of Mme de Vercellis' nephew, Rousseau obtained a position working as a valet/servant in the household of the Count de Gouvon. For a while he was clearly the favorite servant and left to his freedom when not obviously occupied with his duties. His employers saw his intelligence and encouraged his education, notably in Latin and literature, through tutoring with the Abbé de Gouvon, the Count's son.

Another of Rousseau's acquaintances at the time was a young man named Bâcle who inspired Rousseau's sense of adventure and fortune hunting. He began to neglect his studies as well as his duties, and soon fell out of favor with the Count de Gouvon. After being fired he headed back toward Geneva with Bâcle.

Rousseau arrived at Annecy at Mme de Warens' house and bid his former friend farewell. Rousseau dates this return to Mme de Warens at 1731 though there is some evidence it may have been earlier. In the *Confessions* Rousseau describes the reunion with Mme de Warens with effusive emotion.

During this time with Mme de Warens, Rousseau helped her with her horticultural projects and no doubt planted the seeds of the passion for botany that would occupy his final years. He also spent hours reading and generally continuing his education. Throughout his life, Plutarch remained his favorite author. Rousseau truly was the self-taught man, gathering information from varied sources and perfecting his ideas as well as his writing along the way. He describes his thinking and writing practice in the *Confessions*:

> Ideas take shape in my head with the most incredible difficulty. They go round in dull circles and ferment, agitating me and overheating me till my heart palpitates. During this stir of emotion I can see nothing clearly, and cannot write a word; I have to wait. Insensibly all this tumult grows quiet, the chaos subsides, and everything falls into place...If I had known in the past how to wait and then put down in all their beauty the scenes that painted themselves in my imagination, few authors would have surpassed me. (*Confessions,* 113)

Mme de Warens sought advice from friends regarding Rousseau's potential. It was concluded that he would amount to no more than a village priest. Perhaps sensing otherwise, Mme de Warens arranged for Rousseau to be taught at a seminary and there he studied with M. Gâtier, another model for the Savoyard Vicar. Rousseau was not a good student for, as he describes, he suffered under the constraints of instruction. His mind required liberty and he was his own best teacher. Nonetheless, Rousseau was beginning to show his talent for writing and his interest in music; he also wrote the play *Narcisse ou L'Amant de lui-même*.

While at the monastery in Turin studying to become a Catholic, Rousseau had attended the royal mass for the King of Sardinia each morning, not so much for the practice of faith as for the music. His passion for music continued to grow and when sent to the seminary he brought only one book with him: a book of music. He even taught music for a short while but since he was learning it by teaching it, his success was limited. Later he would take a position as a music copier without having much skill at it. Nonetheless, this was to become his sustaining profession. Owning up to his lack of talent in this regard, Rousseau says, "I cannot deny that when I later chose music-copying as my profession I chose the one trade in all the world for which I was least suited" (*Confessions*, 165).

From 1731 to 1732 Rousseau took many walking excursions to obtain new positions, to return to Mme de Warens, to travel to Paris in search of his fame, and occasionally for the mere pleasure of walking. Some of his travels took him to Lyon where Rousseau met his father again. Although Rousseau reports a happy reunion in the *Confessions*, it is more likely that his father disowned him for becoming a Catholic. Isaac Rousseau had remarried but he had no money. Jean-Jacques and his brother had inherited some money from their mother, however, and their father had use of the income from that in their absence. This, Rousseau speculates, kept his father from pursuing him after he ran away from Geneva when he was 16. When Rousseau made arrangements to go to Geneva to claim his inheritance, he discovered it had diminished quite a bit. The experience taught him "one great maxim of morality...to avoid situations which place our duties in opposition to our interests, and show us where another man's loss spells profit for us" (*Confessions*, 62-63).

He spent the winter at Neufchâtel and finally returned to Chambéry and Mme de Warens in 1732. She arranged a post for Rousseau. The temporary post was as secretary in a project of land register of the country to better distribute the imposition of taxes. This was really his first honest living since leaving Geneva.

In 1732, when Rousseau was just 20 years old, Mme de Warens took it upon herself to teach him the ways of women. In becoming her lover, Rousseau was ousting Claude Anet who was living with Mme de Warens at Chambéry and working with her on her horticultural projects. Rousseau describes the three attempting to live a loving threesome, but others have speculated that when Anet died two years later it was of grief at having lost Mme de Warens affections. Rousseau was so captivated by Mme de Warens that he describes their relationship as a necessary relationship: "For it was not, as I have said, a love relationship, but a more real possession, dependent not on the senses, on sex, age, or personal beauty, but on everything by which one is oneself, and which one cannot lose except by ceasing to be" (*Confessions*, 213).

Biography

According to Rousseau, Mme de Warens, or Mamma as he called her, was especially adept at the skills of society. For practical purposes she encouraged Rousseau to learn them although his bent was to reject the proprieties of society in favor of natural virtues. "Mme de Warens knew mankind and was highly skilled in the art of dealing with men, without lying and without indiscretion, without deception, and without offence. But this art was natural to her, she could not teach it; she was better able to put it into practice than to explain it, and of all men in the world I was the least capable of learning it" (*Confessions*, 192). Rousseau spent the next few years attending to his education and enjoying the affections of Mme de Warens.

In 1738 Mme de Warens and Rousseau leased a country house, Les Charmettes. This marked the beginning of a period of happiness for Rousseau. He was continuing with his self-education reading philosophy, science, history, and literature. Voltaire's *Philosophical Letters* helped inspire Rousseau in the direction of philosophy. The two would cross each others paths at a party in 1743 and begin a correspondence a few years later without ever really meeting face to face. Their debate is often used to characterize this period of the Enlightenment. Rousseau also mentions reading other great works in philosophy at this time, including the works of Locke, Descartes, Malebranche, and Leibnitz. He was very systematic in his independent education, working to carefully understand one position before moving on to another.

Rousseau took to thinking himself quite ill with what he called the vapours but might more accurately be called anxiety attacks or hypochondria (*Confession*, 235). Setting off on a journey to find a doctor to cure him, he met some "charming" ladies. (He reports he tried to pass himself off as an Englishman named Monsieur Dudding although he did not speak a word of English.) One of the ladies was a new bride, the other was a woman in her mid-forties and the mother of ten children. It was this second, Mme de Larnage, with whom Rousseau had an affair that he describes as his sole experience of sensual delight.

> If what I felt for her was not precisely love, it was at least so tender a return for the love she showed me, there was so hot a sensuality in our pleasures and so sweet an intimacy in our talk, that it had all the charm of passion without that delirium which turns the head and makes enjoyment impossible. I have only felt true love once in my life, and that was not for her. I did not love her either as I had loved Mme de Warens; and it was for that reason that I was a hundred

times more successful in our intercourse. With Mamma my pleasure was always troubled by a feeling of sadness, by a secret oppression at the heart that I had difficulty in overcoming; instead of congratulating myself upon possessing her, I would reproach myself for degrading her. With Mme de Larnage, on the other hand, I was proud of my manhood and good fortune, and abandoned myself joyfully and confidently to my senses; I shared the sensuality I roused in her, and was sufficiently master of myself to look on my triumph with as much pride as pleasure, and thereby to derive the wherewithal to repeat it. (*Confessions*, 241)

In spite of her invitation and his evident pleasure at doing so, Rousseau decided not to join Mme de Larnage at Bourg-Saint-Andéol. Putting what he viewed as his duty before his pleasure, Rousseau ended the affair and returned to Mme de Warens only to find her ensconced with another man. This "young man," as Rousseau calls him, was actually 6 years older than Rousseau. Rousseau describes the turmoil he felt. His "whole being was thrown completely upside down" at suffering the same fate he had brought to Anet so many years prior (*Confessions*, 249). He was welcome in the home but Mamma grew increasingly cool toward him.

In 1740 Rousseau left for Lyons to become the tutor of M. de Mably's children. M. de Mably was the Chief Provost of Lyons. Rousseau spent a year in this position and although he was generally unsuccessful in tutoring M. de Mably's two sons, it did give him the opportunity to reflect on educational systems. These reflections contributed to his monumental work on education published 22 years later, *Emile*.

One of the two children was named Condillac after his Uncle Abbé de Condillac (1715-1780) author of *Essay on the Origin of Human Knowledge*. Rousseau would later become friends with this famous uncle, but with the nephew Rousseau did the opposite of what he should have done. He says he knew only three methods, "the appeal to sentiment, argument, and anger," none of which is likely to work with young boys.

The philosopher of equality relates an amusing story about his time at M. de Mably's. He took a liking to a wine from Arbois and since it was cloudy he was entrusted to clarify it. In doing so, however, he ruined it to the eye though not to the taste. Once in a while he would take a few bottles to drink on his own. This required some morsel of bread or something to fill his stomach but he found it impossible to obtain. If he sent a lackey to the bakery to buy bread his little thievery would become known and being a gentleman he certainly could not buy it himself. Remembering the words of "a great princess" to the peasants who had no bread, "Well, let them eat cake,"[1] he took it upon himself to buy a cake from a pastry shop. Even this was no easy solution because Rousseau's pretensions required him to enter a confectioners shop only if there was a single person in the shop and that person had pleasant features. When finally he had his cake he returned to drink his wine while reading: "And what pleasant swigs I enjoyed there on my own, while reading a few pages of a novel! For it has always been a fancy of mine to read as I eat when I am on my own; it makes up for the lack of society. I devour a page and a mouthful alternately, and it is as if my book were dining with me" (*Confessions*, 255).

Rousseau ends the happy days of his youth here. While he clearly had moments of happiness, or at least contentment, in subsequent years, he also suffered tremendously from paranoid feelings, suspicions his friends were plotting to destroy him, persecution of his writing, and a feeling of never having truly loved. When reading his laments, one can easily see why he would value pity among the virtues: "After favouring my wishes for thirty years, for the next thirty fate opposed them; and from this continual opposition between my situation and my desires will be seen to arise great mistakes, incredible misfortunes, and every virtue that can do credit to adversity except strength of character" (*Confessions*, 261). The second part of the *Confessions* was written approximately two years after Part I was completed. There is a marked change in tone with the second part as Rousseau feels compelled to record his memories rather than exuberant at recalling times past. He even expresses a desire to simply hide the "misfortunes, treasons, perfidies, and sad, heart-rending recollections" but his desire to defend himself is too strong.

After leaving Les Charmettes and Mamma, Rousseau set out for Paris aiming to make his fortune with a new system of musical notation he had devised using numbers rather than notes on a staff. On 22 August 1742 Rousseau presented his music scheme to the Academy of Sciences. Members of the Academy were intrigued but pointed out the practical limitations of the system. "They decided that it was good for vocal music but bad for instrumental, instead of concluding...that it was good for vocal music, but better for instrumental. As a result of their report the Academy granted me a certificate packed with very fine compliments, between the lines of which anyone could read that in reality they considered my system neither new nor useful" (*Confessions*, 268).

Biography

In 1743 Rousseau took a position as secretary for the French ambassador in Venice. He held this post for only a year and ended on very bad terms with the ambassador. He moved back to Paris in the autumn of 1744 and there met, among others, Thérèse Le Vasseur who was about 22 or 23 at the time. She looked after the linen in the Hotel where Rousseau was staying. Rousseau describes Thérèse as a simple girl from a decent family (though commentators have called her everything including a gossip, a prostitute, and the cause of Rousseau's madness). Her father had worked at the Orléans mint and her mother had a business. When the mint closed and Mme Le Vasseur's business failed, they moved to Paris where they were supported by their daughter.

Rousseau's descriptions of Thérèse are full of admiration if not what he would call love:

> The first time I saw this girl appear at table I was struck by her modest behavior and, even more, by her bright and gentle looks, of which I had never seen the like before....The sympathy of our hearts and the agreement of our dispositions had soon the usual result. She believed that she saw in me an honourable man, and she was not mistaken. I believed that I saw in her a girl with feelings, a simple girl without coquetry; and I was not mistaken either. I declared in advance that I would never abandon her, nor ever marry her. Love, esteem, and simple sincerity were the agents of my triumph; and since her heart was tender and virtuous, I did not need to be bold to be fortunate. (*Confessions*, 309-310)

In Thérèse he found a sort of replacement for Mme de Warens and shared his "docile heart" with her. Rousseau called Thérèse "Aunt"; he had adopted the manner of address that Thérèse and her family called one another when they got together.

Thérèse was soon pregnant and Rousseau searched for a way out of the predicament without dishonoring her or himself. Some dinner companions suggested the Foundling Hospital. "That was the way out I was looking for. I cheerfully resolved to take it without the least scruple; indeed the only scruples that I had to overcome were Thérèse's, and I had the greatest difficulty in the world in persuading her to accept this sole means of saving her honour. But her mother had another fear, that of a fresh embarrassment in the form of a brat, and she came to my aid; Thérèse gave in" (*Confessions*, 322). The child was delivered by a midwife and deposited (with a set of initials on a card) at the Foundling

Hospital. The next year another child was similarly disposed of. In all, Rousseau says that he and Thérèse had 5 children, all deposited at the Foundling Hospital. Rousseau offers a hint of regret in *Emile* but in the *Confessions* his task is simply to tell the truth: "This is one of those essential details which I cannot relate too baldly. For were I to comment on them, I should have either to excuse or blame myself, and here I have no business to do either" (*Confessions*, 320). Rousseau also describes himself as a responsible member of Plato's Republic acting as a citizen and a father. Indeed, he claims to have made the best possible choice for his children and wishes that he had been as fortunate as they in being nurtured and educated by the state. Thérèse, on the other hand, was never at ease with the decision.

In 1749, while walking to visit Diderot in who was confined "to the castle and park of Vincennes" (6 miles from Paris), Rousseau came across the essay contest which he would enter and win, resulting in the *Discourse on the Sciences and Arts*. The contest theme was "Whether the Restorations of the Sciences and Arts has contributed to the purification of morals?" To this Rousseau added the phrase "or the corruption" after "purification" and answered in the negative. His was one of two essays to answer in the negative and he won first prize. More will be said about this essay in Chapter 5; the *First Discourse*, as it is called, was soon published and widely discussed. Rousseau received both acclamation and censure. He counted among his friends some of the greatest thinkers of the day and his own fame was on the rise.

The success of his early writings made him an object of curiosity. He was forced to socialize when he really felt quite ill at ease because of his lack of skill in public proprieties. Following the success and the stir created by the *First Discourse*, Rousseau fell ill. One doctor reported he had 6 months to live. On learning this, he resolved to devote the rest of his time to independence: "...during my convalescence I coolly confirmed the resolutions I had taken in my delirium. I renounced for ever all plans for fortune and advancement. I determined to spend the little time I had still to live in independence and poverty, and put all the strength of my soul into breaking the fetters of prejudice, courageously doing what seemed to me right, without in the least worrying what men might think" (*Confessions*, 337). In other words, Rousseau sought to live by the principles he had laid out in the *First Discourse*. He turned his back on the trappings of society opting instead for simplicity in dress and deportment. He also turned his back on public opinion, opting not to be swayed by so fickle a force, he would follow virtue instead. Rousseau marks this as a sort of conversion to truth that was not well received by his contemporaries. In particular, he suspected his friends of conniving to destroy him. The following quotation reveals the bitterness Rousseau felt as well as the irony of his concern for his reputation while abandoning public opinion as a measure of his morality:

> If I had shaken off the yoke of friendship as well as that of public opinion, I should have accomplished my purpose, the greatest perhaps, or at least the most serviceable to virtue ever conceived by moral man. But whilst I was trampling underfoot the senseless opinions of the vulgar herd of so-called great and so-called wise, I allowed myself to be enslaved and led like a child by so-called friends, who were jealous at seeing me strike out alone down a new road and, whilst appearing to be much concerned for my happiness, in fact used every endeavour to make me look ridiculous, and began by striving to disgrace me so that afterwards they could succeed in robbing me of my reputation. (*Confessions*, 338)

Meanwhile, Rousseau's interest in music was also advancing. Rameau had set Voltaire's play *La Princesse de Navarre* to music. Rousseau was commissioned to polish the piece but unfortunately was left unacknowledged when the piece was presented. Rousseau counted among his friends Diderot, Condillac, and Grimm. Diderot and d'Alembert undertook *Le Dictionnaire encyclopédique* and asked Rousseau to write some articles on music which he says he wrote "very badly in a great hurry."

Rousseau finished his opera *Le Devin du Village (The Village Soothsayer)* in 1752 and it was played at Court at Fontainebleau with, as he reports, some success. King Louis XV was so impressed that he wanted to give Rousseau a pension (the king's mistress, Mme de Pompadour had played a role in the opera), but Rousseau was terrified of appearing before the King in part because his awkwardness and inability to speak spontaneously. He fled instead. Diderot was displeased with Rousseau's response and this appears to be the first argument between the two friends. *The Village Soothsayer* brought Rousseau more social success. He also says the opera marks a period in his life and "is mixed up with that of the relationships I had at the time." Diderot and Grimm were Rousseau's only chosen friends yet after the success of his opera he perceived a distancing: "After this success I no longer found in Grimm or Diderot or – with a few exceptions – in the other literary men of my acquaintance, the cordiality, the sincerity, and the pleasure in my company that I had hitherto believed them to feel" (*Confessions*, 360).

Rousseau's *Letter on French Music*, published in 1753, was taken as an insult after the success of *Soothsayer*. Rousseau preferred Italian music to French. This letter, and a similar attack on music published later that year, took on a bombastic style that left no question regarding Rousseau's utter disdain for the state of musical arts in France at the time. As a result of this national insult, Rousseau was denied some of the rights and privileges of a composer, including a free pass to the Opera. Indeed, there was even talk of forcing him into exile but that fate would wait for another day. Rousseau finally gave up hope of fame via music and, to match his newly adopted simple lifestyle, he resumed his career as music copyist.

The Dijon Academy in 1753 proposed the "Inequality of Mankind" as the theme of its essay contest. Rousseau was taken by the theme and once again entered but felt he had very little chance of winning because of the content of his essay. His essay, known as the *Discourse on the Foundation and Origin of Inequality among Mankind* (often called the *Second Discourse*), was published in 1755. The stir it created was slightly less than the *First Discourse* but its historical importance cannot be overstated. In preparation for writing, Rousseau took a trip to Saint-Germain and wandered in the forests imagining what it must have been like in primitive times. His reflections led him to contrast the man of nature and the man of society:

> I demolished the petty lies of mankind; I dared to strip man's nature naked, to follow the progress of time, and trace the things which have distorted it; and by comparing man as he had made himself with man as he is by nature I showed him in his pretended perfection the true source of his misery. Exalted by these sublime meditations, my soul soared towards the Divinity; and from that height I looked down on my fellow men pursuing the blind path of their prejudices, of their errors, of their misfortunes and their crimes. Then I cried to them in a feeble voice which they could not hear, 'Madmen who ceaselessly complain of Nature, learn that all your misfortunes arise from yourselves!' (*Confessions*, 362)

Inequality would be the enduring theme for his work as well as his life until his death 25 years later. Alas, he felt that few people in Europe could understand his *Discourse on Inequality*. At about this same time

Biography

Rousseau completed an article for *L'Encyclopédie* on *Political Economy*.

On a journey to Geneva in 1754, Rousseau stopped to see Mme de Warens. Mamma, as he called her, had sunken quite low. Eight years later, in 1762, she died. Rousseau reflected on their different fates in the *Confessions*, hers was one of poverty while his was one of loneliness: "After spending a life of plenty, Mamma was fated to experience all the miseries of want and discomfort, in order that she might leave the world with less regret; and I, by a concatenation of every sort of evil, was doomed one day to be an example to all who, solely out of love for justice and the public good, and strong in their innocence alone, might dare openly to speak the truth to men..." (*Confessions*, 214).

When he arrived back in Geneva, Rousseau returned to Protestantism in part because of the welcome he received and in part because of his desire to reclaim the rights of Citizen. True to what the Savoyard Vicar proclaims, Rousseau declared that the Gospel was "the same for all Christians" and where differences in fundamental truths appeared these could be explained by humans arrogantly trying to explain what they were not capable of understanding. Everything else about religion, according to Rousseau, rested "with the sovereign alone in each country to settle the form of worship and the unintelligible dogma as well" (*Confessions*, 365). The next chapter analyzes this radical view of personal interpretation of faith in conjunction with the *Profession of Faith of a Savoyard Vicar*, a central passage from Rousseau's *Emile*.

Rousseau hoped to return to Paris merely to pack things up and return once more to Geneva with Thérèse. He planned to go back to Geneva in the following spring but Mme d'Épinay gave him the use of a cottage instead. He moved into the Hermitage, as it was called, in April of 1756, leaving Paris "never to live in a town again." He stayed at the Hermitage until 15 December 1757 when he became the guest of Lord Marshal (M. de Luxembourg) at Montmorency. Rousseau's move to the Hermitage marked the beginning of a very productive period of his life if also a period filled with as much turmoil.

When D'Alembert published an article on *Geneva* in *L'Encyclopédie* arguing, among other things, that Rousseau's beloved birth-place ought to have a theater (in part so that the works of Voltaire might be performed there), Rousseau felt compelled to make a public response. In this response, *Letter to M. D'Alembert on the Theater* published in 1758, Rousseau argued for censorship much as Plato had done in the *Republic*. The preface of Rousseau's *Letter to d'Alembert* contained a public announcement of his break with Diderot. The latter had been Rousseau's dearest friend but as the years wore on, the two grew increasingly distant in their philosophical positions. No doubt Diderot was also disappointed that Rousseau would take such a stance against the theater when he hoped to obtain success with some of his writings for the theater. Whether or not it was because of Rousseau's *Letter to D'Alembert*, Geneva did not build a theater. Rousseau, for his part, felt the disapprobation of his peers but also the courage that comes from speaking the truth on behalf of the common good.

Simultaneously with the *Letter to M. D'Alembert on the Theater* Rousseau had been working on his great novel *Julie*, more commonly known as *La Nouvelle Héloïse* and also titled *Letters of two lovers who live in a small town at the foot of the Alps*. The first version of *Julie* was finished in 1757, the final six part version was finished in 1758 and published in 1761.

Rousseau was yearning for love; he claims to have never loved Thérèse though he surely admired her, even calling her "the best of women" (*Reveries*, 155). She was, however, illiterate and although they were faithful companions for 33 years (and finally married in 1768), Rousseau's desire for love was for a love that would overflow the bounds of his heart. Indeed, for Rousseau love was wrapped up with suffering. Ever the romantic, he longed for the love that he wrote about in *Julie*. "How could it be that, with a naturally expansive nature for which to live was to love, I had not hitherto found a friend entirely my own, a true friend – I who felt so truly formed to be a friend? How could it be that with such inflammable feelings, with a heart entirely molded for love, I had not at least once burned with love for a definite object? Devoured by a need to love that I had never been able to satisfy, I saw myself coming to the gates of old age, and dying without having lived" (*Confessions*, 396-397). The imaginative exercise that resulted in *Julie* was, in his own words, Rousseau's effort to "give some sort of expression to my desire to love which I had never been able to satisfy, and which I now felt was devouring me" (*Confessions*, 401).

Rousseau found this love in the person of Mme d'Houdetot. In the midst of writing *Julie*, he was ripe for a romantic swoon and Mme d'Houdetot merely provided the impetus. He had known her as a child and he was becoming closer friends with her lover M. de Saint-Lambert, who was in the military. Mme d'Houdetot and Mme d'Epinay were sisters-in-law and Rousseau saw the former at parties during his stay at the Hermitage.

Mme d'Houdetot rented a house near the Hermitage and came to visit Rousseau one afternoon on horseback. The delirium of the love letters between Julie and her lover together with seeing Mme d'Houdetot arrive in such a romantic fashion was enough to break him. Rousseau calls her his "first and only love" but it was unrequited; Mme d'Houdetot was in love with Saint-Lambert. Her name was Sophie and she was the model for the Sophie of *Emile*. Rousseau recounts the passion he felt in her presence as well as the natural beauty that unfolded around her.

> One evening when we supped together alone we went for a walk in the garden in the loveliest moonlight. At the bottom of the garden was a largish wood through which we went to find a pretty plantation adorned with a newly made cascade for which I had given her the idea. Immortal memory of innocence and bliss! It was in that wood, sitting with her on a grass bank beneath an acacia in full flower, that I found a language really able to express the emotions of my heart. It was the first and only time in my life, but I was sublime, if such a word can describe all the sympathy and seductive charm that the most tender and ardent love can breathe into the heart of a man. What intoxicating tears I shed at her knees! What tears I drew from her in spite of herself! (*Confessions*, 413-414)

Rousseau's meetings with Mme d'Houdetot were at La Chevrette (Mme d'Épinay's home) and continued for approximately three months. Mme d'Épinay watched with, according to Rousseau, growing indignation and rage. Mme d'Épinay treated Mme d'Houdetot badly while also treating Rousseau well, thereby dividing Rousseau's affections. Mme d'Houdetot chastized Rousseau for his impropriety; her lover had been informed of Rousseau's attentions to his beloved and scandal was soon to follow.

Rousseau claims he broke with Diderot because the latter had told Saint-Lambert, Mme d'Houdetot's lover, some of what Rousseau had told him in confidence. Diderot could not be trusted. Similarly, Rousseau accused Grimm, Mme d'Epinay, Tronchin, and others of conspiring to bring him down. (He also thought Thérèse's mother, Mme Le Vasseur, was conniving with Diderot and others as he was writing *Confessions*.)

> The secret accusations of treachery and ingratitude were spread more cautiously, and were for that reason even more effective. I knew that they charged me with heinous crimes, but I never could learn what they alleged them to be. All that I could deduce from public rumour was that they could be reduced to these four capital offences: (1) my

retirement to the country; (2) my love for Mme d'Houdetot; (3) my refusal to accompany Mme d'Épinay to Geneva; (4) my leaving the Hermitage. (*Confessions*, 456)

In 1762 Rousseau published his treatise on education, *Emile,* and his influential work in political philosophy, *Social Contract.* The latter had been brewing in Rousseau's thought since his stint as secretary to the French Ambassador to Venice in 1743-1744 under the title *Political Institutions.* He describes his purpose as discerning "What is the nature of the government best fitted to create the most virtuous, the most enlightened, the wisest, and, in fact, the best people, taking the word 'best' in its highest sense?" (*Confessions*, 377). As we will see in Chapter 4, governments must suit the material conditions of the people.

Both *Emile* and the *Social Contract* induced violent consequences. *Emile* was banned and Rousseau was condemned, largely for the profession of faith of the *Savoyard Vicar* in book four of *Emile.* Rousseau had thought the Jesuits and later the Jansenists and Philosophers were plotting against him and keeping *Emile* from being published. The *Social Contract* was forbidden publication in Paris. Word was sent that he would be arrested and prosecuted for what he had said in *Emile*; he was forced to leave. He hastily said goodbye to Mme de Luxembourg and the Marshal and departed. Both texts were burned in Geneva. He spent the next several years in exile, forced out of each new resting place until finally going to England as the guest of David Hume in 1766. In the mean time he had been excommunicated and renounced his Genevan citizenship. When recounting the events subsequent to the publication of the *Social Contract* and *Emile*, Rousseau remarks that the attacks must be against him and not the works because the principles in the works had appeared in his earlier writings to no great disapproval. Indeed, the profession of faith of the Savoyard Vicar is no different than the faith Julie expresses as she dies. Similarly, the *Discourse on the Origin of Inequality* was as challenging (if not more so) than the *Social Contract.* Rousseau took these public displays of disapproval as part of the work of the conspirators he thought were trying to destroy him.

Throughout all of this emotional turmoil, Rousseau was also suffering from a physical ailment that forced him frequently to have to wear a catheter. He was finally diagnosed with an enlarged prostate. No doubt this physical ailment as well as his suspicions of conspiracy caused him to suffer a great deal during the years he should have been enjoying the fame and accolades due such a masterful writer and theorist.

While the *Confessions* ends with his exile, there are two other volumes of autobiographical works. The first is often called *Dialogues* but its full title is *Rousseau, Judge of Jean-Jacques*. It was written between 1772 and 1776 and is comprised of three dialogues between "Rousseau" and the "Frenchman." The former in this case is a character rather than the author. "Rousseau" and the "Frenchman" discuss the work of "Jean-Jacques." The Frenchman has not read Jean-Jacques' work at the start of the dialogues but reads it by the end. "Rousseau" has read (but is not the author of) Jean-Jacques' work. This format allows Rousseau (the author) to defend himself against unfair accusations against his work. The splitting of personalities, however, has also led many to speculate about the extent of Rousseau's paranoia. For himself, he wanted posterity to know the truth and that explains his attempt to place the manuscript of the completed *Dialogues* on the alter at the Cathedral of Notre Dame. Finding the gates to the alter closed, he instead gave the manuscript to Condillac who simply treated it like another of Rousseau's philosophical works, making comments and suggestions for revisions. The *Dialogues* was published in 1782 but with many omissions. The complete version did not appear until 1958.

The last autobiographical work is the *Reveries of the Solitary Walker* which appeared in 1782 as did the first six books of the *Confessions*. The last six books of the *Confessions* were published just before the start of the French Revolution in 1789. *Reveries* consists of ten reflections of morning walks during the last two years of Rousseau's life. The last three "walks," as they are called, were written during the winter and spring before his death in 1778. The most sustained theme in the *Reveries* is that of truth. Rousseau took as his motto a saying from Juvenal: *vitam impendere vero* or "to devote one's life to the truth." The lie he had told in his youth – blaming Marion for the theft of a ribbon he committed – continued to haunt him to his dying day. This incident provides the setting for Rousseau's examination of truth and falsehood. He sought a reliable rule by which to tell when to tell the truth or not. The question is complicated by whether the rule itself is infallible.

Late in his life, Rousseau took up botany. His passion for this new pursuit is evidenced in this passage from *Reveries of the Solitary Walker*:

> I could have written...about every grass in the meadows, every moss in the woods, every lichen covering the rocks – and I did not want to leave even one blade of grass or atom of vegetation

without a full and detailed description....Nothing could be more extraordinary than the raptures and ecstasies I felt at every discovery I made about the structure and organization of plants and the operation of the sexual parts in the process of reproduction... (*Reveries*, 84)

Also in *Reveries*, Rousseau distinguishes between the self-love or natural inclination for self-preservation and *amour-propre* or vanity. The latter is the cause of our unhappiness; it is that which gives rise to a foolish pride resulting in jealous hatred of others. Love of self, by contrast, brings us back to the "sweet and happy life" for which we are born (*Reveries*, 131). The distinction between love of self and vanity arguably forms the foundation of all of Rousseau's moral and political writings. As we will see in the next chapter, Rousseau's *Emile* is an attempt to articulate the program of education that best fosters the true man of nature in his love of self. Similarly, the social contract might be understood as an ideal society wherein vanity or pride (*amour-propre*) have no place.

On 2 July 1778, after an early morning walk and his usual breakfast, Rousseau died with Thérèse by his side. He was 66 years old. He had spent the last of his days enjoying his new love of botany in relative isolation at the private residence of the Marquis de Girardin at Ermenonville. He was buried nearby but his remains were moved to the Pantheon in Paris in 1794.

Endnotes

1. This is commonly attributed to Marie Antoinette. Rousseau wrote it before she arrived in France in 1770. The *Confessions*, recalling 1740, is the only record; he does not mention Antoinette by name.

3
Education

In the 18th century, education, especially among the aristocracy, entailed a rigid, disciplined study of books as soon as a child was able to read. Prior to that time, the child was likely tended to by a wet nurse. The aristocracy often sent their infants to live with peasants in the country, in part to avoid the filth of the city. There was also a tendency to wrap babies tightly in swaddling clothes so as to prevent them from harming themselves. In this context, Rousseau's writings on education were quite radical. But even more radical were his thoughts regarding political philosophy, human nature, and faith. Thus, his system of education in *Emile* might be read as a system of philosophy as well as a proposal for rearing a child.

Rousseau's *Emile* is part novel, part treatise. A long time friend, Mme de Chenonceaux, had been begging Rousseau for a system of education for her son (*Confessions*, 381) and in undertaking the project Rousseau drew on his own experience as a self-taught man as well as his brief stint as a tutor to two children of M. de Mably. Throughout *Emile*, Rousseau critiques the work on education by philosopher John Locke. Rousseau's system is aimed at raising a child according to nature as opposed to raising a child for society. More importantly perhaps, Rousseau's education aspires to develop the character as much as or more than the intellect. The book is divided into five sections which correspond to five major periods of childhood and young adulthood.

Book I Infancy

Before beginning his recommendations, Rousseau suggests two things that ought to be considered for any scheme: 1) "Is it good in itself?" and 2) "Can it be easily put into practice?" (*Emile*, 3). These are guiding principles for his educational system but might also be used to judge other aspects of society. Certainly Rousseau used these two questions to analyze social morals or standards of propriety both in his writings and in his adopted lifestyle.

Another guiding precept of most of Rousseau's thought is that "God makes all things good: man meddles with them and they become evil" (*Emile*, 5). Rousseau distinguishes Nature from Habit. You cannot train both the man and the citizen, he says, because according to the current system, Nature is pitted against society: "Our wisdom is slavish prejudice, our customs consist in control, constraint, compulsion. Civilized man is born and dies a slave. The infant is bound up in swaddling clothes, the corpse is nailed down in his coffin. All his life long man is imprisoned by our institutions" (*Emile*, 11). Rousseau's educational system is more than a reform; it is a completely new approach. It attempts to educate the man of nature and thereby create the ideal citizen in contrast to the man of society. "The natural man lives for himself; he is the unit, the whole, dependent only on himself and on his like. The citizen is but the numerator of a fraction, whose value depends on its denominator; his value depends upon the whole, that is on the community" (*Emile*, 7-8). The father "owes men to humanity, citizens to the state" (*Emile*, 19). Rousseau describes three types of education used in raising the man of nature: "The inner growth of our organs and faculties is the education of nature, the use we learn to make of this growth is the education of men, what we gain by our experience of our surroundings is the education of things" (*Emile*, 6).

The real purpose of education is character rather than knowledge. To this end, Rousseau recommends experience and practice rather than books (see also *Julie*, 110). The "one science" the child is to learn is "the duties of man"; the tutor does not give "the precepts" for the "scholar" must discern them for himself. In rearing the child, however, moderation is the key. That being said, it is clear that "We begin to learn when we begin to live; our education begins with ourselves, our first teacher is our nurse" (*Emile*, 10). Rousseau thus begins his treatise on education by addressing the mother. The mother is given milk to feed her child and she watches over the education of the child early on. (The widow, after all, is at the mercy of the child she raised.) Rousseau is credited with commanding women to nurse their own children and abandon swaddling clothes. The latter constrained the natural movement and freedom of the child. The former challenged the widely accepted practice among the aristocracy of sending babies out to nurse with peasant women. Rousseau thought that women nursing their own children might also decrease the infant mortality rate.

Although the child's first teacher is its nurse or mother, a tutor will soon be needed unless the father is able to undertake this task himself. (Rousseau presumes the teacher, whether tutor or father, will be male. Until Book V, the student is likewise male.) The tutor should be young enough to "become a child himself" and can only educate one child at a time. Ideally, the tutor will be chosen before the child is born. Perhaps more importantly, the tutor ought to accept no remuneration for his services. Rousseau views the work of the teacher and the soldier as callings; when undertaken for pay these professions violate the maxim "to avoid situations which place our duties in opposition to our interests" (*Confessions*, 61-62). Rousseau himself plays the part of the tutor to his imaginary student.

Picking a student is just as important for the tutor as picking a tutor is for the child. Rousseau recommends an ordinary child from temperate climates. He clearly prefers a European child in part because of the temperate climate. Extremes, whether in climate, intelligence, or wealth, are a disadvantage. For the purposes of his treatise, Rousseau adopts an imaginary pupil who is French. Rousseau calls this imaginary pupil Emile and tells us Emile comes from a good family.

> I have therefore decided to take an imaginary pupil, to assume on my own part the age, health, knowledge, and talents required for the work of his education, to guide him from birth to manhood, when he needs no guide but himself. This method seems to me useful for an author who fears lest he may stray from the practical to the visionary; for as soon as he departs from common practice he has only to try his method on his pupil; he will soon know, or the reader will know for him, whether he is following the development of the child and the natural growth of the human heart. (*Emile*, 20)

Rousseau calls Emile an orphan not because his parents are necessarily dead but because while the parents are honored, it is the tutor who is obeyed. Indeed, Rousseau includes two conditions for the education of the child, one of which is that by relinquishing the duties to educate their child, Emile's parents give their rights also. The tutor inherits those rights as we see so clearly when Emile is ready to be married. Additionally, the tutor and student must not be separated except by "mutual consent." Their fates are one; they must love one another.

An interesting side note in Book I is Rousseau's tirade against medicine. "I do not deny that medicine is useful to some men; I assert that it is fatal to mankind" (*Emile*, 25). Even when Mme de Warens was experimenting with pharmacological properties of plants, Rousseau expressed a disdain and disinterest in this branch of science. His interest in botany was purely for the pleasure of identifying plants not in obtaining their medicinal uses. Nonetheless, his contempt for medicine does not quite fit with his relentless search for a doctor in his youth and into adulthood. One might surmise that Rousseau was attracted by illness but repulsed by remedies. Perhaps the more apt interpretation, however, is that it is society that creates the need for medicine; natural man, living in isolation, would rarely be ill: "Men are not made to be crowded together in ant-hills, but scattered over the earth to till it. The more they are massed together, the more corrupt they become. Disease and vice are the sure results of over-crowded cities. Of all creatures man is least fitted to live in herds. Huddled together like sheep, men would very soon die. Man's breath is fatal to his fellows. This is literally as well as figuratively true" (*Emile*, 30).

Book II Learning Morals by Experience

Book II of *Emile* focuses on teaching the child morals. These lessons should never be instructed but instead should be learned through experience. Rousseau introduces it by saying it is a discussion of pain and pleasure. He also spends a fair bit of time toward the end of Book II on the development of the senses. It is important to note that Rousseau would not have us teaching about good and evil at an age when the child is not able to understand it. In fact, he recommends waiting until the child is quite old to speak of duty, and much older still (around 15 years old) to speak of religion. This is why Rousseau starts his lesson on teaching morality by teaching about the development of the physical person. The body must be strong for to the mind to be strong as well.

Pain, or the ability to bear pain, then becomes the first lesson on the way to becoming a moral person. The development of strength leads to the development of a sense of self and thus to becoming a moral being (this is echoed toward the end of Book II as well). Being able to bear pain and having the strength to do more for oneself makes one independent but also requires the development of the sense of when and how to use strength. According to Rousseau, this development marks the beginning of self-conscious existence. An enduring self is necessary for the capability to feel joy or sorrow and thus to be considered a moral being. Implied in this is the existence of other human beings. Rousseau does not think an isolated individual is moral; morality requires association with others. He issues an imperative to emphasize this point: "Men, be kind to your fellow-men; this is your first duty, kind to every age and station, kind to all that is not foreign to humanity" (*Emile*, 50).

Next Rousseau discusses the source of human misery which is also the topic of his *Second Discourse*. Rousseau's formula for misery or happiness is: "Every feeling of hardship is inseparable from the desire to escape from it; every idea of pleasure from the desire to enjoy it. All desire implies a want, and all wants are painful; hence our wretchedness consists in the disproportion between our desires and our powers. A conscious being whose powers were equal to his desires would be perfectly happy" (*Emile*, 51-52). In other words, the key to happiness is in decreasing the distance between our ability and our desire. We must learn to want what we have the power to obtain for ourselves. Since nature provides humans with the power to satisfy the desires needed for self-preservation, and since these are the only desires primitive man has, it follows that in the state of nature there is an equilibrium between desire and power such that man is free from misery. Misery results from the needs created by imagination because the latter "enlarges the bounds of possibility for us, whether good or ill, and therefore stimulates and feeds desires by the hope of satisfying them" (*Emile*, 52).

From this conception of the creation of human misery, Rousseau derives a rule for education which aims at avoiding the inculcation of unnecessary needs and desires in the child. Using freedom rather than power as the greatest good, Rousseau argues that Emile will be truly free because he "desires what he is able to perform, and does what he desires" (*Emile*, 56). Included in this rule is a rejection of superfluous human institutions; human institutions often raise contradictory desires in the hearts of man while also encouraging weakness and dependence rather than strength and independence. Hinting at a resolution to the problem of misery caused by a widening gap between power and will, Rousseau appeals to law. His system of education aims at restoring to man the liberty deprived because of inequality resulting from dependence on others:

> There are two kinds of dependence: dependence on things, which is the work of nature; and dependence on men, which is the work of society. Dependence on things, being non-moral, does no injury to liberty and begets no vices; dependence on men, being out of order, gives rise to every kind of vice, and through this master and slave become mutually depraved. If there is any cure for this social evil, it is to be found in the substitution of law for the individual; in arming the general will with a real strength beyond the power of any individual will. If the laws of nations, like the laws of nature, could never be broken by any human power, dependence on men would become dependence on things; all the advantages of a state of nature would be combined with all the advantages of social life in the commonwealth. The liberty which preserves a man from vice would be united with the morality which raises him to virtue. (*Emile*, 58)

To follow the order of nature in education, one must "Keep the child dependent on things only" (*Emile*, 58). Rousseau instructs us to follow nature – let the child run when he wants to run and sit when he wants to sit. The activities of the child are instincts; thwarting nature leads to capricious desires.

Recall that Rousseau cautions against teaching the child moral rules before he reaches the age of reason. Until that time, the child simply cannot understand the words "duty" and "obligation." The tutor must instead use words the child does understand in order to prepare him to one day take up his role as a moral being with social relations. Strength and weakness, necessity and constraint are the tools for developing the child's moral sense at this early age. Because the child is not yet moral, it follows that he ought not to be punished for wrongdoing. Instead, the tutor ought to use experience to teach the child that what he does is unwise or harmful. By way of example, Rousseau uses the story of Emile breaking a window. Rather than punish the child, Emile should be made to sleep in the room with the broken window. He will soon learn that his behavior was foolish and, as he catches cold from the draft, he will understand it as harmful as well. Emile will remember this experience and be more careful in the future. A similar example has Emile challenging the tricks of a conjurer at a local fair. When Emile and his tutor figure out the trick of the magician, they go to the fair to demonstrate it. The conjurer turns the tables on them and changes the trick. Emile is surprised and embarrassed that his trick does not work. Rousseau uses this example to teach about magnetism, cause and effect, as well as vanity and respect. The tutor and student were endangering the livelihood of the conjurer.

Contrary to his argument in the *Discourse on the Origin of Inequality*, in *Emile* Rousseau discusses the importance of property and how best to teach the child about the rights and obligations of a property owner. Rousseau's discussion of property here, however, is interwoven with a discussion of charity. This mingling of the two themes lends a more nuanced notion of justice than might be evident at first glance.

Since our first feelings and instincts are directed toward our self or our self-preservation, it follows, according to Rousseau, that "the first notion of justice springs not from what we owe to others, but from what is due to us." This concept distinguishes Rousseau's method of education from that of his contemporaries in that it asserts the priority of teaching children about their rights before they can understand their duties to others. Further, since things cannot defend themselves, "the first idea he needs is not that of liberty but of property..." (*Emile*, 73). Like all of the lessons taught by Rousseau's tutor, this lesson is taught by experience. The child should be given something of his own. Rousseau offers the following example: The child will want to plant and work the land after watching the gardener. The tutor will help the child to plant a bean seed. Each day they will observe its growth and the tutor will explain how the bean plant belongs to the child. In explaining "belong," the tutor will "show him how he has given his time, his labour, and his trouble, his very self to it..." The property is "part of himself which he can claim against all the world." The child must take care, however, that the land he sows was not sown by someone else first, as Emile learns the hard way (*Emile*, 74).

The property owner also has an obligation to charity and Rousseau instructs the tutor to give of his time and service as well as money. The oppressed, says Rousseau, need protection rather than money (*cf. Julie*, 249). When money is given it ought to be given by the tutor not the child, for, as Rousseau explains, "Alms-giving is the deed of a man who can measure the worth of his gift and the needs of his fellow-men"

(*Emile*, 79). Clearly a child is incapable of assessing the needs of others; if the child does give the money then he thinks that charity is child's play and that there is no need to practice it when he is an adult. Money also has little meaning for the child. Generosity is giving what is dear to oneself. Rousseau means that the tutor is to teach the child by example. When the time is right, the tutor explains that he is merely the master of the money; he has made a promise to care for the poor, this is a condition of ownership. Rousseau contrasts his proposal with that of philosopher John Locke who encourages us to get the child to give in the understanding that in giving one will get back more in return. Rousseau sees this sort of usury as failing to teach generosity. A child often gives what is useless to him or her or what he or she expects to get back.

Having established the relations of property and gained a rudimentary understanding of rights, the child is ready to build some of the foundation for morality. Rousseau argues that this foundation is in the senses and begins his explanation with the epistemological faculties:

> Although memory and reason are wholly different faculties, the one does not really develop apart from the other. Before the age of reason the child receives images, not ideas; and there is this difference between them: images are merely the pictures of external objects, while ideas are notions about those objects determined by their relations. An image when it is recalled may exist by itself in the mind, but every idea implies other ideas, when we image we merely perceive, when we reason we compare. Our sensations are merely passive, our notions or ideas spring from an active principle which judges. (*Emile*, 85)

Next, Rousseau cautions against teaching a child to read too early. This logically follows the above because words are merely images with no value unless they are accompanied by an idea of that which is symbolized. Reading has no clear use for the child and may lead the child into falsehood because he does not have the experience to give him the ideas that correspond to the images or words. As Rousseau explains, "Since everything that comes into the human mind enters through the gates of sense, man's first reason is a reason of sense-experience. It is this that serves as a foundation for the reason of the intelligence; our first teachers in natural philosophy are our feet, hands, and eyes. To substitute books for them does not teach us to reason, it teaches us to use the reason of others rather than our own; it teaches us to believe much and know little" (*Emile*, 106-107). Rousseau's point in this discussion is twofold. First, he contends that experience is superior to book-learning. Rousseau would have Emile unaware of books until his early teens. Nonetheless, Rousseau is confident that Emile will learn to read well by the age of 10 out of necessity precisely because the tutor does not care if he is able to read by 15. In other words, "What we are in no hurry to get is usually obtained with speed and certainty." The second facet of Rousseau's rejection of reading in favor of knowledge gained through experience is that the body must be exercised so that the mind may be. The similarity with Plato's *Republic*, where guardians are exercised before learning rhetoric or philosophy, is striking. Similarly, the child's physical activity ought not to be constrained, by clothing or convention.

Following from this example of reading, it is clear that children ought to learn only that which is clearly valuable for use or enjoyment. The task is to arouse the desire to learn rather than teach unnecessary things. The tutor should also pay attention to the body and ensure that it remains strong and independent. Rousseau says, for instance, that children should wear summer clothes in winter to get accustomed to the weather and be hearty in the cold. They should drink cold water when they are hot and they should sleep in uncomfortable beds so that they can sleep anywhere. The hard life "increases our pleasant experiences; and easy life prepares the way for innumerable unpleasant experiences" (*Emile*, 112). Part of living this hard life is also confronting illness. Rousseau debates the relative merits of having his pupil inoculated against the small pox. He concludes that for Emile it is better to let "nature" take its course. Although he is not making a general statement about inoculation, he is saying that it is of little importance one way or another if Emile is inoculated.

Since Emile learns by doing and since knowledge comes through sense experience, Rousseau offers a systematic discussion of the development of each of the senses. One sense that cannot be "turned off" is touch. Emile ought to be comfortable in the dark; he will use his sense of touch to navigate the darkened room. The "natural fear" of the dark is caused by ignorance rather than nature. Our natural instinct for self-preservation, however, puts us on our guard against those things we imagine when we hear sounds in the dark that we cannot explain. Emile will not have the ignorance that gives rise to fear of the dark because he will have plenty of experience using touch to replace the knowledge of sight deprived by the darkness. Emile will even play games in the dark so that he will look forward to it rather than recoil from it.

Touch, then, is "the sense which best teaches us the action of foreign bodies upon ourselves, the sense which most directly supplies us with the knowledge required for self-preservation" (*Emile*, 122). Sight is the sense that is most closely linked to the activity of the mind in that it is difficult to distinguish between what we see and what we judge. Thus, Rousseau says that it takes a long time to learn how to see properly.

Hearing is next and Rousseau adds voice to his discussion of this sense. This addition allows him to note the three types of voice (the singing, the speaking, and the expressive) which leads him to conclude that music also should be taught as play and not as discipline.

Taste provides the stimulus for a discussion of not only oral sensation but also cultural or national ceremony. Holding to his rule that desire and power ought to be in equilibrium for human happiness, Rousseau argues that tastes should be simple. This simplicity in taste allows for easy adaptation to new sensations and thus greater tolerance for different cultures. More complex tastes become "fancies" and are difficult to overcome. The rule in eating, as in everything, is to follow nature. Let the child "eat and run and play as much as they want." Nature will tell him when he is full (*Emile*, 143). (Rousseau also notes that humans have a natural proclivity to eat vegetables; he quotes Plutarch regarding how appalling it must have been when the first person decided to eat the sheep that licked his hands. Plutarch adds that humans eat not those animals that kill other animals but those that serve us.) Finally, the sense of smell precedes the sense of taste, in order to give warning. It is thus, like sight is to touch, more closely linked to the instinct for self-preservation.

The last sense to be developed is common sense but this sense is much more complex than the other five. The development of common sense marks the change from childhood to adulthood because it marks the movement from knowledge obtained through the senses to reason. Rousseau explains:

> In the following books I have still to speak of the training of a sort of sixth sense, called common-sense, not so much because it is common to all men, but because it results from the well-regulated use of the other five, and teaches the nature of things by sum-total of their external aspects. So this sixth sense has no special organ, it has its seat in the brain, and its sensations which are purely internal are called percepts or ideas. The number of these ideas is the measure of our knowledge; exactness of thought depends on their

clearness and precision; the art of comparing them one with another is called human reason. Thus what I call the reasoning of the senses, or the reasoning of the child, consists in the formation of simple ideas through the associated experience of several sensations; what I call the reasoning of the intellect, consists in the formation of complex ideas through the association of several simple ideas. (*Emile*, 145)

The tutor has taken care not to treat Emile as a man before he is capable of reason. He is still a child but Rousseau's system is designed to provide the proper basis for later development of morality. Thus far, Emile – a product of Rousseau's system of education – does not distinguish between work and play. Nor does he perceive any men as unequal to any others. He will be a leader of nature and other men. Emile eschews habit because that makes a person lazy. The only habit he will adopt as a child is the difficult submission to necessity. As an adult, his habit is the even more difficult submission to reason.

Book III Usefulness as a measure of value

Book III focuses on the third stage of childhood. The pupil has not yet reached puberty but is approaching it. Emile is about 12 or 13 years old. Rousseau mentions that the pupil's progress in geometry is a test of intelligence, he is beginning to discern between the useful and the useless. The tutor skillfully arouses the child's curiosity and lets him solve the problems himself. In this way he develops the dexterity of mind that will serve him well into adulthood. The tutor must be careful not to substitute authority for reason, that is, the child must figure things out for himself and not be told the solution to a problem. In this new stage of education, the pupil learns that usefulness is the measure of value: "Hitherto we have known no law but necessity, now we are considering what is useful; we shall soon come to what is fitting and right" (*Emile*, 155). This is simply a step in the development of the knowledge of good and evil, moral ideas.

Using an allusion to Robinson Crusoe, Rousseau argues that our study should focus on that which has a "natural attraction" for us or to which our "instinct impels us." Our earth is our island which is one reason the philosophy of primitive peoples is directed toward the split between the heavens and the earth. They address their experience just as Emile should. "Let us transform our sensations into ideas, but do not let us jump all at once from the objects of sense to objects of thought. The latter are attained by means of the former. Let the senses be the only guide for the first workings of reason. No book but the world, no teaching but that of fact. The child who reads ceases to think, he only reads. He is acquiring words not knowledge" (*Emile*, 156).

Rousseau is careful also to avoid arousing any sort of feeling or taste in the child. He is too young for the passions. In general, Rousseau is concerned with teaching the truth and avoiding every sort of confusion. Introducing feeling into teaching at this stage can confuse ideas and lead the child into error. Since prejudice and opinion is easily learned, Rousseau takes every measure to avoid them by fostering the right development of reason and judgment. Even more fundamentally, the task of the teacher is to foster a desire to learn and thereby let the child determine the subject of the learning. The teacher is not to fill the child's head with useless knowledge about which the child has no experience.

Thus, study continues to be learning from experience. The teacher and student even make their own instruments with which to study physics. Chemistry is taught through the acids and minerals in wine. (Rousseau remarks in a footnote that Paris wines are rarely free of lead. This is because the wine is poured into measures on counters made of lead. Some of the wine inevitable spills. What is more, he says, "It is strange that so obvious and dangerous an abuse should be tolerated by the police. But indeed well-to-do people, who rarely drink these wines, are not likely to be poisoned by them" (*Emile*, 174).) Among the many benefits of this practical approach is that the child will gain further strength of body as he learns. Recall that Rousseau urges the perfection of bodily strength and skill simultaneously with mental development.

Up to this point, Rousseau has said nothing about playmates or companions for Emile. Indeed, Emile is raised in relative isolation from his peers. With the exception of occasional running races to perfect ability, Emile has had no interaction with society. This is done so as to protect him from corrupting social morals but, more importantly, to teach him to be self-sufficient. Emile will have the strength and industry to provide for his simple needs. When he was younger those needs were met by a mother or a nurse. As he grows older he begins to do things for himself. When the child can foresee his needs, he is beginning to know the value of time and he evinces progressing intelligence. Similarly, the child does what is good not because he is told it is good but because he recognizes it as good himself. Usefulness, then, is the measure of goodness at this stage in Emile's education and will remain a test of actions into adulthood.

Eventually, of course, Emile will learn to read, either by himself or with the help of the tutor. Rousseau carefully picks out the first book Emile will read:

> Since we must have books, there is one book which, to my thinking, supplies the best treatise on an education according to nature. This is the first book Emile will read; for a long time it will form his whole library, and it will always retain an honoured place. It will be the text to which all our talks about natural science are but the commentary. It will serve to test our progress towards right judgment, and it will always be read with delight, so long as our taste is unspoilt. What is this wonderful book? Is it Aristotle? Pliny? Buffon? No; it is *Robinson Crusoe*. (*Emile*, 176)

But our own Emile, aka Robinson, will eventually have needs that he cannot meet by himself; he will learn the industrial arts. In other words, Emile will have a need for human companionship. The teacher should show his student first the usefulness of human companionship for industry. The moral component of this social intercourse must come later.

The tutor can take this opportunity to teach his pupil about the value of work and economics. Working together, a hundred people can produce enough for twice their number but inevitably there will be some who do not perform their share of work. Others will have to work harder to make up for the idlers. This is why Rousseau says it is imperative that every member of society, rich or poor, work. As Emile is now ready to comprehend business, the tutor can instruct him in the art of exchange. As he explains, exchange should be taught according to the real value (usefulness) of objects and not the false or imaginary value that the wealthy put on objects. This is especially evident in the case of art. As Rousseau explains, "The value set by the general public on the various arts is in inverse ratio to their real utility. They are even valued directly according to their uselessness. This might be expected. The most useful arts are the worst paid, for the number of workmen is regulated by the demand, and the work which everybody requires must necessarily be paid at a rate which puts it within the reach of the poor" (*Emile*, 178). Artists, as opposed to artisans, work for the rich and put a high price on their work. The wealthy value these things because they are out of reach of the poor not because they are useful. Similarly, at a fine party the tutor asks his student how many people were used to prepare the feast. The simple question awakens the child to all the labors of the poor that go to help the rich live a lavish lifestyle. Rousseau issues a caution that our students not adapt to this theory of value. All efforts are wasted if Emile, like other scholars, takes on the airs of the wealthy.

Having something (tools) that is not useful to us but is useful to someone else (and vice versa) necessitates exchange. Rather than having 10 people each do 10 different things to meet their needs, it is more efficient to have each of the 10 work at that which is best fitted to his talents. These 10 men form a society. As Emile will soon learn, there can be no exchange without some standard of measurement. But this standard relies on some conventional notion of equality. Although conventional equality may be of things, if it is of men then there must be some law to ensure it. Thus, from society for industry to exchange, from exchange to conventional equality, Rousseau has derived the need for civil government. These relations are explored more thoroughly in the next chapter on Rousseau's politics. For this stage in Emile's education, let us assume a conventional equality between things rather than men.

Money is the clearest example of a standard of comparison between different sorts of products. The ruler has sole right of coining money. Rousseau instructs the reader to teach the simple lesson that money is used in exchange but not how money is the corrupting influence of society or the "source of all the false ideas of society" (*Emile*, 182). That knowledge is beyond the student's grasp according to Rousseau; it is understood only by wise men who discern the difference between reality and appearance.

Although he has no need of the money, it is important for Emile to learn a trade. (Rousseau would certainly not have Emile be an idler in society.) Emile is free to choose his own trade with the exception of embroiderer, gilder, polisher, musician, actor, or author. He must pursue an honest trade that is not contrary to humanity. Honesty entails usefulness. Rousseau would choose the trade of carpenter for Emile because manual labor is closest to the state of nature and least dependent on the fickle winds of fate. Both tutor and student should be apprenticed in the trade. Later, when Emile is traveling, he will find his sustenance through the employment of this skill. Indeed, even master carpenters will be amazed at his proficiency.

Aside from the obvious benefits of learning a trade, Emile will also

Education

gain one other very valuable asset. In occupying the hands, Emile is temporarily saved from the workings of his imagination. This is not to say that his mind becomes inactive but rather that his passions do not cloud his concerns. Rousseau explains,

> If I have made my meaning clear you ought to realize how bodily exercise and manual work unconsciously arouse thought and reflection in my pupil, and counteract the idleness which might result from his indifference to men's judgments, and his freedom from passions. He must work like a peasant and think like a philosopher, if he is not to be as idle as a savage. The great secret of education is to use exercise of mind and body as relaxation one to the other. (*Emile*, 197)

The child is complete; we are ready to discuss the man. Emile is a capable thinker and a skillful worker. The task that remains is to teach him how to live in society and to love. He must also learn how to control the passions and use them to enhance reason rather than counter it.

Book IV The Passions

Emile has reached the age to learn judgment, especially the judgment of good and bad. The key to doing so is the passions and chief among the passions is love of self or self-love. Self-love is the only passion that is born with us and the passion from which all others stem. It is always good and clearly upholds nature's order. In particular, since the first rule of nature is self-preservation, self-love instinctually directs the individual to what is helpful to his or her well-being and deters him from what is harmful. Self-love changes from an instinct to a feeling when intention is involved.

The second passion is for others. As Rousseau explains, "The child's first sentiment is self-love, his second, which is derived from it, is love of those about him; for in his present state of weakness he is only aware of people through the help and attention received from them" (*Emile*, 209).

The distinction between self-love and *amour-propre* (variously translated as selfishness or vanity, and confusingly as self-love) is one of the central tenets of Rousseau's philosophy. Rousseau explains:

> Self-love, which concerns itself only with ourselves, is content to satisfy our own needs; but selfishness [or vanity], which is always comparing self with others, is never satisfied and never can be; for this feeling, which prefers ourselves to others, requires that they should prefer us to themselves, which is impossible. Thus the tender and gentle passions spring from self-love, while the hateful and angry passions spring from selfishness. (*Emile*, 209)

In other words, the love of self or self-love is part of human nature and it contributes to our self-preservation. Humans are by nature good and the natural man has few needs that are met through his own power. *Amour-propre* considers the opinions of others and multiplies the individual's needs making him jealous, greedy, competitive, and generally wicked. It follows from this distinction that suffering is our own making. In education, it is not difficult to see where selfishness enters and becomes pride or vanity (the former in great minds, the latter in lesser ones). As love has to be mutual, we must also inspire love. In order to do so, the student must be "more worthy than the rest" and this is what turns his attention to his fellows in comparison. While these passions were not present in the child, they spring forth in the young man. The training must foresee this and curb them.

The first people your pupil will be drawn to are like himself in what they have experienced and what they enjoy. Thus his liking for them is more out of self-love than other-love. Since the development of the passions is primarily aimed at social intercourse and companionship, Rousseau includes some practical advice together with his more abstract discussion of human nature. He instructs us not to tell lies to children. When their curiosity strikes, answer them in a plain speech, without making the subject sound mysterious or tell them not to ask such questions (as this latter has been practiced with trivial things, they will not question further). When a child perceives there is something to hide or something to be modest about, his curiosity will not rest until he knows what it is. Speak simply about everything so that the child will not suspect there is more to know. This is especially the case with matters pertaining to the opposite sex.

Morality is not present when a person's consciousness extends only to one's self. When consciousness or imagination extends beyond the self, then morality begins to arise – first as the sentiments and then as "the ideas of good and ill." Pity, according to nature, is the first sentiment. It appears with the realization that others suffer as oneself.

Education

"Hence it follows that we are drawn towards our fellow-creatures less by our feeling for their joys than for their sorrows; for in them we discern more plainly a nature like our own, and a pledge of their affection for us. If our common needs create a bond of interest our common sufferings create a bond of affection" (Emile, 218-219). With Emile, encouraging all of the delicate passions such as pity, kindness, and beneficence is not a difficult task because his education up to this point has prepared him for this precise moment. In others students, however, one must take care not to allow envy, hatred, greed, and all the other evil passions to take root and flourish. This will be no easy task in a society in which vanity is the rule of the day.

Rousseau sums up the preceding lessons with the following maxims: (1) "It is not in human nature to put ourselves in the place of those who are happier than ourselves, but only in the place of those who can claim our pity" (*Emile*, 221). (2) "We never pity another's woes unless we know we may suffer in like manner ourselves" (*Emile*, 222). (3) "The pity we feel for others is proportionate, not to the amount of the evil, but to the feelings we attribute to the sufferers" (*Emile*, 223).

Emile is to witness the sufferings of others but, in order to avoid hardening him, he must be shown these sights only infrequently. This will allow him, on turning back to himself, to experience his own simple life as pleasant; that is, because he has avoided the woes others experience he is happy. Notice that the pity Emile feels is not a haughty pity but a sincere fellow-feeling.

Once he is capable of affection he is also aware of the affection for others. Rousseau describes friendship as a contract. To have a friend one must be a friend; affection might be unrequited but friendship cannot be. Emile is gradually learning which of his sentiments may be universalized. He is, in other words, learning about humankind. What he learns is that individuals are by nature good but society makes them bad. Humans create their own sufferings and vices by falling prey to prejudices and public opinion. A look through history reveals the truth of this position.

Finally, Emile is ready to study justice. Justice contributes to the common good more than any other virtue. Reason and self-love compel us to love humankind; this love is the love of justice. The key to understanding this conception of justice is to remember that loving humanity is simply self-love turned outward. To accomplish this end, we should ensure that self-interest is kept at bay. In addition, Emile must practice the social virtues:

Mothers and nurses grow fond of children because of the care they lavish on them; the practice of social virtues touches the very heart with the love of humanity; by doing good we become good; and I know of no surer way to this end. Keep your pupil busy with the good deeds that are within his power, let the cause of the poor be his own, let him help them not merely with his money, but with his service; let him work for them, protect them, let his person and his time be at their disposal; let him be their agent; he will never all his life long have a more honorable office. How many of the oppressed, who have never got a hearing, will obtain justice when he demands it for them with that courage and firmness which the practice of virtue inspires; when he makes his way into the presence of the rich and great, when he goes, if need be, to the footstool of the king himself, to plead the cause of the wretched, the cause of those who find all doors closed to them by their poverty, those who are so afraid of being punished for their misfortunes that they do not dare to complain? (*Emile*, 254)

Emile has learned about physics and chemistry, economics, history, and morality, it is now time to teach him about faith. Up to this point Emile has little knowledge of his own soul or of God precisely because he is too young to understand it. "The obligation of faith assumes the possibility of belief" (*Emile*, 264). Rousseau is cautious about teaching "the truth" to someone who is not yet capable of understanding it, doing so gives rise to error.

Emile will not be attached to any religious sect but instead will be given the means of deciding for himself. Rousseau defends his method of faith education by claiming that "no child who dies before the age of reason will be deprived of everlasting happiness." While this commonly held belief was usually meant to mean that the child should not be without faith by the age of 7, Rousseau means that children are not yet ready at 15. Until a man can reason on his own, his faith is more a product of geography than belief. Holding religious teachings until later in life will not lead the child into damnation. As Rousseau says, "Reason tells that man should only be punished for his wilful faults, and that invincible ignorance can never be imputed to him as a crime. Hence it follows that in the sight of the Eternal Justice every man who would believe if he had the necessary knowledge is counted a believer, and that there will be no unbelievers to be punished except those who have closed their hearts against the truth" (*Emile*, 265).

Education

Rousseau offers his own story of conversion from Calvinism to Catholicism "for a morsel of bread" as evidence. This leads to the *Profession of Faith of a Savoyard Vicar*. The priest helped the young man who was on the brink of moral death, to regain his love of self. As part of the education of Emile, the *Profession of Faith* serves as an example of how to talk to the student about religion.

Profession of Faith of a Savoyard Vicar

When Rousseau was about 16 years old he met a Savoyard priest by the name of Abbé Jean Claude Gaime. M. Gaime and a M. Gatier, whom Rousseau met while at a seminary to which Mme de Warens had sent him, together inspired the Savoyard Vicar and his profession of faith (though it is Rousseau's confession as well). The *Profession of Faith of a Savoyard Vicar* is the most overtly metaphysical piece of Rousseau's works. Perhaps the most notable (and controversial) aspect of this confession of faith is that Rousseau argues that individuals themselves ought to interpret their faith, and more importantly their morality. The duties of Church are to discuss the religious ceremonies because they pertain to culture more than God. The background for this controversial claim is yet another controversy. The Enlightenment philosophers, or *philosophes*, were staunchly irreligious and their ideas were constantly being challenged by the Catholic Church. Rousseau enters the debate with a sort of third position. He rejects the materialism of the *philosophes* while also rejecting the dogmatism of the Church. Our independence in moral judgment comes from our ruling conscience which is given by God. Like so much of Rousseau's educational system, the *Profession of Faith of a Savoyard Vicar* emphasized independence and questions authority.

Rousseau begins the *Profession of Faith* with the challenge to materialism and proceeds to the faculty of judging so as to argue for the existence of God.

The love of truth was the guiding philosophy for the Savoyard Vicar and to this end he begins by noting that self-evident truths are those truths that cannot not be believed. Anything derived from self-evident truths must also necessarily be true. The first truth is personal existence: "I exist, and I have senses through which I receive impressions" (*Emile*, 278). The next difficulty however is whether one is aware of one's own existence through sensation or independently. Since it is clear that there is a difference between what is perceived and what is sensing or perceiving, it follows that there is a difference between oneself (as a perceiving subject) and other objects or bodies. Matter describes the particles of these other objects. There is thus a difference between feeling and judging. The former is perceiving while the latter is comparing. The mind produces comparisons, such as greater and smaller or number (one, two, etc), when sensations occur. For instance, I see my hand and I count to five. In perceiving two things, the relation between them is not perceived. That relation is judgement but it is not also the case that we are passive in receiving sensations.

In perceiving things through the senses one perceives matter and deduces "all the essential properties of matter from the sensible qualities which make me perceive it, qualities which are inseparable from it" (*Emile*, 280). Neither rest nor motion are among these essential qualities though rest is the natural state of things. In order to move, something must cause the motion. There are two kinds of motions: acquired and spontaneous or voluntary motion (external and internal respectively). Since nothing can move unless there is a will to move it, the Vicar concludes with the first article of faith, that there is a will to the universe.

> In a word, no motion which is not caused by another motion can take place, except by a spontaneous, voluntary action; inanimate bodies have no action but motion, and there is no real action without will. This is my first principle. I believe, therefore, that there is a will which sets the universe in motion and gives life to nature. This is my first dogma, or the first article of my creed. (*Emile*, 282)

The second article of faith derives from the fact that motion appears to be in accordance with laws and this implies not just a will but an intelligence. Thus, the Vicar adds a teleological argument to the cosmological argument above:

> I am like a man who sees the works of a watch for the first time; he is never weary of admiring the mechanism, though he does not know the use of the instrument and has never seen its face. I do not know what this is for, says he, but I see that each part of it is fitted to the rest, I admire the workman in the details of his work, and I am quite certain that all these wheels only work together in this fashion for some common end which I cannot perceive....Whether matter is eternal or created, whether its origin is passive or not, it is still

Education

> certain that the whole is one, and that it proclaims a single intelligence; for I see nothing that is not part of the same ordered system, nothing which does not co-operate to the same end, namely, the conservation of all within the established order. This being who wills and can perform his will, this being active through his own power, this being, whoever he may be, who moves the universe and orders all things, is what I call God. (*Emile*, 284-285, 286-287)

In brief, the two arguments for the existence of God work together: (1) I perceive that objects are moved; (2) movement is either caused by another or caused by the object itself; (3) nothing can move unless there is a will to move it; (4) inanimates do not have a will and thus (5) must be moved by another. So, (6) the universe too must have a mover. (7) The universe operates according to laws; (8) the mover who wills thus must be a mover with intelligence. (9) This intelligent mover who "orders all things" is called God.

That God exists is quite different than understanding the metaphysical attributes of God; indeed, the Vicar says that he can make no claim about the nature of God because God does not appear to the senses. From the arguments above, however, we can surmise that God has both intelligence and will. God must also be powerful in order to create and order the universe. The final attribute mentioned by the Vicar is kindness as a consequence of the other three.

God creates man as the "lord of the earth." He tames animals and makes use of the elements of the earth for his purpose and through his industry. He also controls the world through contemplation. Through a recognition of the chaos and evil among mankind, the Vicar is lead to the soul. "While I meditated upon man's nature, I seemed to discover two distinct principles in it; one of them raised him to the study of the eternal truths, to the love of justice, and of true morality, to the regions of the world of thought, which the wise delight to contemplate; the other led him downwards to himself, made him the slave of his senses, of the passions which are their instruments, and thus opposed everything suggested to him by the former principle" (*Emile*, 289). In other words, the Vicar echoes a theme Rousseau has previous used in devising the instruction of Emile: One is free when one listens to reason; one is enslaved when one is controlled by the passions. With the recognition of a human soul as the source of evil, the Vicar distinguishes substances. Matter is divisible and extended; it thus cannot think. The non-extended soul thinks.

The nature of the soul is best described as freedom but Rousseau, through the Vicar, is careful not to give the soul complete license. "No doubt I am not free not to desire my own welfare, I am not free to desire my own hurt; but my freedom consists in this very thing, that I can will what is for my own good, or what I esteem as such, without any external compulsion. Does it follow that I am not my own master because I cannot be other than myself?" (*Emile*, 291) In other words, the soul is bound by rules of nature, the primary rule being self-preservation. When our passions tempt us, our conscience keeps us in check. However, when conscience fails to restrain our actions, then God ensures that our misuse of freedom for the sake of evil is limited so as to not disturb the "general order." Summing up the cause of evil, the Vicar says, "O Man! seek no further for the author of evil; thou art he. There is no evil but the evil you do or the evil you suffer, and both come from yourself. Evil in general can only spring from disorder, and in the order of the world I find a never-failing system. Evil in particular cases exists only in the mind of those who experience it; and this feeling is not the gift of nature, but the work of man himself" (*Emile*, 293).

The triumph of the wicked convinces the priest that there must be some universal harmony; that is, the problem of evil is resolved first through human free will and secondarily through a conception of universal harmony. If there appears no justice in the deeds of the wicked, God's order ensures justice elsewhere: "Justice uses self-inflicted ills to punish the crimes which have deserved them" (*Emile*, 296). Goodness is what creates order and justice preserves it. Humans are naturally good and God only wills what is good. In addition, the existence of two substances (in humans, body and soul) allows that the death of one (body) but does not entail the death of the other (soul). However, the Vicar admits not knowing if the soul is immortal. It follows from this, according to the Vicar, that God's justice, if it be retributive, is a justice in this life; a life in hell is thereby ruled out. God demands that we give a report of all that God has given us.

Human justice, on the other hand, "consists in giving to each his due." Having thus laid out the principal truths derived from the fact that we are perceiving beings, we now turn to rules of conduct/morality. These rules are writ on one's heart by nature; there is no need to turn to "higher philosophy," simply turn inward. "I need only consult myself with regard to what I wish to do; what I feel to be right is right, what I feel to be wrong is wrong; conscience is the best casuist; and it is only when we haggle with conscience that we have recourse to the subtleties of argument. Our first duty is towards ourself....Conscience is the voice of the soul, the passions are the voice of the body" (*Emile*, 298).

The Vicar argues that man is naturally good for, if man were naturally evil, then goodness would be contrary to nature. In addition, our own desire for happiness is not independent of the desire for the happiness of others. When we see others suffer we pity them and thus suffer as well. This instinct leads us to desire the happiness of others insofar as their happiness does not interfere with our own.

The Vicar's (and Rousseau's) normative moral theory is Natural Law. In part this theory is substantiated by an examination of other nations. The Vicar notes that although customs vary, every culture has the same conception of justice and the same principles of morality. This universality of morality is guided by conscience for it is conscience that judges actions to be good or evil.

> Whatever may be the cause of our being, it has provided for our preservation by giving us feelings suited to our nature; and no one can deny that these at least are innate. These feelings, so far as the individual is concerned, are self-love, fear, pain, the dread of death, the desire for comfort....man is by nature sociable....But the motive power of conscience is derived from the moral system formed through this twofold relation to himself and to his fellow-men. To know good is not to love it; this knowledge is not innate in man; but as soon as his reason leads him to perceive it, his conscience impels him to love it; it is this feeling which is innate. (*Emile*, 303)

This ends the first part of the *Profession of Faith*. The second part is more dialogue and less soliloquy. Rousseau, continuing to use himself as a character in the dialogue, asks what the Vicar thinks of Scripture. The priest says that each individual is capable of interpreting scripture. This was one of the most scandalous doctrines from the *Profession of Faith of a Savoyard Vicar*. Understandably the idea that the authority of the Church should be questioned contributed to the book being banned and burned. Rousseau himself was exiled and the house in which he stayed was stoned. In fact, the Vicar actually claims that interpretive doctrines show man's arrogance and confuse the ideas of reason. The Vicar replaces Church doctrine and dogma with reason and an individual's conscience, both being gifts from God. The key is to listen to God through "the heart of man" rather than try to put words or rituals to it; words or rituals will necessarily bear the mark of the nation or culture from which they sprung. The form of worship is not in need of revelation, it simply relies on custom and discipline. As the Vicar says, "Do not let us confuse the outward forms of religion with religion itself. The service God requires is of the heart; and when the heart is sincere that is ever the same" (*Emile*, 310). The authority of God speaks to reason. We should not, therefore, substitute the authority of man for the authority of God. To judge a religion, one must look to the lives of practitioners rather than what is written in books.

Rousseau next undertakes a direct critique of the Catholic Church by having his Vicar question the Church's authority: "'Our Catholics talk loudly of the authority of the Church; but what is the use of it all, if they also need just as great an array of proofs to establish that authority as the other seeks to establish their doctrine? The Church decides that the Church has a right to decide. What a well-founded authority!'" (*Emile*, 320). Extending this critique, the Vicar calls into question the very sacredness of scripture saying it also is a product of culture. The unbeliever will want to know who wrote the scriptures and how it was preserved; he or she will also inquire about the fate of those who are unaware of or reject scripture. All of this is said as an argument for religious toleration. In a footnote, Rousseau says there ought to be no distinction between civil toleration and religious toleration (*Emile*, 327). It is immoral (because intolerant) to claim that someone is damned because they are outside the Church. These sentiments are forcefully reiterated later in the *Emile* when Rousseau is discussing the education of girls and, in particular, what girls should be taught regarding faith.

> Whether a virgin became the mother of her Creator, whether she gave birth to God, or merely to a man into whom God has entered, whether the Father and the Son are of the same substance or of like substance only, whether the Spirit proceeded from one or both of these who are but one, or from both together, however important these questions may seem, I cannot see that it is any more necessary for the human race to come to a decision with regard to them than to know what day to keep Easter, or whether we should tell our beads, fast, and refuse to eat meat, speak Latin or French in church, adorn the walls with statues, hear or say mass, and have no wife of our own. Let each think as he pleases; I cannot see that it matters to any one but himself; for my own part it is no concern of mine. But what does concern my fellow-creatures and myself alike is to know that there is indeed a judge of human fate, that we are all His

children, that He bids us all be just, He bids us love one another, He bids us be kindly and merciful, He bids us keep our word with all men, even with our own enemies and His; we must know that the apparent happiness of this world is naught; that there is another life to come, in which this Supreme Being will be the rewarder of the just and the judge of the unjust. (*Emile*, 411-412)

Reverting back to the autobiographical, the Vicar advises "the young man" to return to his homeland and practice the religion of his father, that is, he tells Rousseau to return to Geneva and be a Calvinist. (Recall that Rousseau had converted to Catholicism, in part, because it provided charity when he needed it.) He also instructs Rousseau to always speak according to conscience without regard for the opinion of others (*Emile*, 331). The confession/discussion stops there. Rousseau comments that the *Profession of Faith* is not included here as a normative or prescriptive statement on religion but rather as an example of how to talk and reason with Emile about religion. Later in his life, Rousseau did admit that the *Profession of Faith of the Savoyard Vicar* was also his own profession of faith (*Reveries*, 55).

From Faith to Social Intercourse

We have reached a point with our pupil where we can speak to him (to his heart) in a different manner. He has found "a real motive for doing good." Rousseau compares his pupil with that of others. His pupil, not having been indoctrinated, is not bored with questions of theology. Instead, he is just opening his mind and heart to the Divine. "To be just in his own eyes and in the sight of God, to do his duty, even at the cost of life itself, and to bear in his heart virtue, not only for the love of order which we all subordinate to the love of self, but for the love of the Author of his being, a love which mingles with that self-love, so that he may at length enjoy the lasting happiness which the peace of a good conscience and the contemplation of that supreme being promise him in another life, after he has used this life aright" (*Emile*, 333).

From this, Rousseau shifts into a discussion of the first sexual impulses, finding a mate, and procreation. This discussion is the primary or underlying focus of rest of the book. It is time, according to Rousseau, to stop treating the pupil as a pupil and start treating him as a man. As with all lessons, we are also cautioned against lecturing the

Education

young man; virtue must be taught gradually over the course of a life rather than forced on a person through lecture. You must prepare the way before you can reason with your pupil. This is also the part of the treatise on education that begins to look much more like a novel as we hear stories of Emile's emerging drives and the wanderings of his imagination.

Rousseau is concerned that, when given a free reign, imagination will lead Emile into danger. In order to avoid this potentiality, he suggests intense physical activity – whether work or play. Physical activity, as opposed to merely mental activity, has the added benefit of working off the excess energy gotten from Emile's musings. Rousseau specifically suggests hunting as the occupation to check Emile's imagination. Hunting provides the sport and the chase that Emile seeks and thus "serves to delay a more dangerous passion." Rousseau is not, however, endorsing a youth spent in killing animals. On the contrary, there is a tone of disdain in his suggestion but reason seems to prevail as hunting is presented as the closest approximation to the sexual conquest that will soon occupy Emile's aspirations. Rousseau's advice is unmatched in beauty and complexity. He simultaneously sings the pleasure of sex, the obligation of virtue, and the depravity of licentiousness:

> ...I maintain that if instead of the empty precepts which are prematurely dinned into the ears of children, only to be scoffed at when the time comes when they might prove useful, if instead of this we bide our time, if we prepare the way for a hearing, if we then show him the laws of nature in all their truth, if we show him the sanction of these laws in the physical and moral evils which overtake those who neglect them, if while we speak to him of this great mystery of generation, we join to the idea of the pleasure which the Author of nature has given to this act the idea of the exclusive affection which makes it delightful, the idea of the duties of faithfulness and modesty which surround it, and redouble its charm while fulfilling its purpose; if we paint to him marriage, not only as the sweetest form of society, but also as the most sacred and inviolable of contracts, if we tell him plainly all the reasons which lead men to respect this sacred bond, and to pour hatred and curses upon him who dares to dishonor it; if we give him a true and terrible picture of the horrors of debauch, of its stupid brutality, of the downward road by which a first act of misconduct leads from bad to

worse, and at last drags the sinner to his ruin; if, I say, we give him proofs that on a desire for chastity depends health, strength, courage, virtue, love itself, and all that is truly good for man – I maintain that this chastity will be so dear and so desirable in his eyes, that his mind will be ready to receive our teaching as to the way to preserve it; for so long as we are chaste we respect chastity; it is only when we have lost this virtue that we scorn it. (*Emile*, 345-346)

Emile must learn how to live with his fellow men. He knows the ways of humankind, now he must learn about individual humans. In particular, Emile must find a companion. Rousseau introduces his young man to society with the aim of finding a suitable companion. The tutor will describe the virtuous companion for Emile and in doing so create a sort of image of what Emile is to look for. This will turn him away from superficial or misguided attractions. Thus while Emile searches for a woman to match his heart, he also becomes accustomed to society. In addition, having a goal or aim to social interactions keeps Emile from being easily led astray or corrupted by the false pretenses of that society. Rousseau comments that Emile is docile precisely because, after so many years of education in the fashion Rousseau describes, in his freedom he consents to the constraints of reason.

Now that Emile is a man and interacting in human institutions, it would be wise to distrust instinct. This reverses the order of childhood. In adulthood, instinct must be carefully controlled and supplanted with reason. Rousseau does not separate mastering one's sexual urges from participating in society.

Rousseau offers a description of Emile in society. He is polite and affectionate but does not seek attention. In some ways, Emile does not fit in society and yet he is well received. He does not fit because he neither practices nor knows the social proprieties and yet he is well liked because he is recognized as a man of virtue. One of the occupations of society that becomes Emile's study is the vicissitudes of taste. Taste is "merely the power of judging what is pleasing or displeasing to most people" though it does not follow that taste is the majority opinion.

Taste deals only with things that are indifferent to us, or which affect at most our amusements, not those which relate to our needs; taste is not required to judge of these, appetite only is sufficient...Taste is natural to men; but all do not possess it in the same degree, it is not developed to the same extent in every one; and in every one it is liable to be modified by a variety of causes. Such taste as we may possess depends on our native sensibility; its cultivation and its form depend upon the society in which we have lived. (*Emile*, 365)

Taste is dependent on culture, social institutions, politics, as well as age, sex, and character. The most important element to his conception of taste is that true beauty is in nature and the works humans judge beautiful are mere imitations of nature. Rousseau scorns the trifles of the wealthy that they value so highly. These trifles are always beyond necessity and contrary to nature, "luxury and bad taste are inseparable." The true man of taste needs freedom not wealth. Rousseau muses about his own life if he were wealthy. He would have few servants because he would want to walk to shops himself, both for the exercise and for the better price. He would not build a large house because he would not want to be bounded by location. When you are rich, your home is where your money is. He would have simple tastes and simple possessions as "abundance is the cause of want." He would never make people aware of inequalities in wealth because of his attire. He would, in short, continue to live in such a way that his desires and his powers are not greatly separated; and, he would share his wealth for "monopoly destroys pleasure" (*Emile*, 382).

With this connection to nature, it becomes clear that good taste is associated with good morals. The development of taste is particularly important for the interaction between men and women. Fostering Emile's sense of beauty is merely an element of Rousseau's discussion of sexual urges. "My main objective in teaching him to feel and love beauty of every kind is to fix his affections and his taste on these, to prevent the corruption of his natural appetites, lest he should have to seek some day in the midst of his wealth for the means of happiness which should be found close at hand" (*Emile*, 370). Rousseau is furthering Emile's education so that when his heart is ready to look, it will look rightly.

Book IV ends with a turn to Sophie, the ideal woman of nature. Emile and his master will seek to find Sophie. Rousseau argues that true virtue cannot be found in the cities, especially Paris and London. Sophie is not to be found there "with all your noise and smoke and dirt, where the women have ceased to believe in honour and the men in virtue" (*Emile*, 383).

Education

Book V Emile and Sophie

Rousseau describes writing the fifth book of *Emile* at the Chateau at Montmorency in "a continuous ecstasy" (*Confessions*, 483). The ecstasy was inspired by Mme d'Houdetot whom Rousseau describes as his only true love. (One of Mme d'Houdetot's names was "Sophie.") Book V begins with a description of Sophie, the ideal woman of nature, to match Emile, the ideal man of nature. Rousseau does not stop at merely introducing the pair, he guides their courtship up until the marriage day.

The first half of this last book of *Emile* focuses on the education of women, or more specifically, the education of Sophie. Like Emile, Sophie must be prepared to adopt all the responsibilities of her sex "to enable her to play her part in the physical and moral order" (*Emile*, 384). Unlike other theorists of his day, Rousseau did not accept that women and men should be educated similarly. On the contrary, he held that their similarities were due to the species and their differences were due to sex. The first difference between men and women in their moral relations is that the "man should be strong" and the "woman should be weak and passive." Woman's strength is in her charms which she should use to compel man to exert his; one clear way of doing so is by resisting. Rousseau describes courting much like a military attack: "Whether a woman shares the man's passion or not, whether she is willing or unwilling to satisfy it, she always repulses him and defends herself, though not always with the same vigour, and therefore not always with the same success. If the siege is to be successful, the besieged must permit or direct the attack. How skillfully can she stimulate the efforts of the aggressor! The freest and most delightful of activities does not permit any real violence..." (*Emile*, 386).

In order to please man, woman ought to make herself agreeable to him and avoid provocation. Another difference of the sexes is that the "stronger party seems to be master, but is as a matter of fact dependent on the weaker" (*Emile*, 387). In other words, because of her ability to refuse the man's sexual advances as well as her other forms of manipulation, the woman is actually stronger than the man. The man must depend on the woman for his sexual satisfaction, thus he must work to please her. "Men have found that their pleasures depend, more than they expected, on the good will of the fair sex, and have secured this goodwill by attentions which have had their reward" (*Emile*, 388).

Rousseau speculates that if women were educated like men then they will have less influence over men and thus men will truly be the masters. Moreover, he says,

> Women do wrong to complain of the inequality of man-made laws; this inequality is not of man's making, or at any rate it is not the result of mere prejudice, but of reason. She to whom nature has entrusted the care of the children must hold herself responsible for them to their father. No doubt every breach of faith is wrong, and every faithless husband, who robs his wife of the sole reward of the stern duties of her sex, is cruel and unjust; but the faithless wife is worse; she destroys the family and breaks the bonds of nature; when she gives her husband children who are not his own, she is false both to him and them, her crime is not infidelity but treason. ... [She] is robbing his own children of their inheritance." (*Emile*, 388-389)

Evidently, the virtues of women are different from the virtues of men. Rousseau critiques Plato for assigning the same task to both sexes; doing so ignores these natural differences. (He also argues against Plato that it is the good father who makes the good citizen.) One outcome of these different virtues is that whereas men are to follow the truth and disdain public opinion, women must follow the truth and be concerned with public opinion: "what people think of her matters as much as what she really is" (*Emile*, 392-393). This also helps to explain why women have more knowledge of taste than men.

The early education of a female is to fit her for her future profession of wife and mother in accordance with nature. This profession also involves some coquetry which will focus her education differently than the male's. Naturally, girls love decorative clothing. They seek to be admired. As a child she plays with dolls as a way to practice for when she will become her own doll. She dresses and decorates the doll as she will one day dress and decorate herself.

Like Emile, Sophie's education must develop her physical body as well as her mental and moral self. Whereas boys develop the body for strength, girls develop the body for grace. But the development of grace should also accord with nature. Rousseau criticizes corsets because they confine nature and "it is not a pleasant thing to see a woman cut in two like a wasp" (*Emile*, 395).

In order to prepare her for her role as a woman, Rousseau recommends the girl be subject to more restraint in childhood. His aim is to produce the docility a woman requires to be subject to man and public opinion. Notice how this contrasts with Emile's education. Emile was instructed not to accept anything on authority; Sophie, on the other hand, is trained not only to accept authority but to create the conditions of obedience that will make her subordinate her own opinion. But Rousseau would not have women be passive. He claims that women have the natural gift of cunning that will allow them power over the men such that the stronger are really the weaker.

Foreshadowing contemporary discussions of rapport versus report or care versus justice, Rousseau claims that there is a natural distinction between the social intercourse of men and women. Men are helpful and women caressing: "A man seeks to serve, a woman seeks to please." This is true of both words and actions. Whereas a man speaks the truth with no care of public opinion, a woman, while not lying, speaks in order to give pleasure. Rousseau further explains:

> You should not check a girl's prattle like a boy's by the harsh question, 'What is the use of that?' but by another question at least as difficult to answer, 'What effect will that have?' At this early age when they know neither good nor evil, and are incapable of judging others, they should make this their rule and never say anything which is unpleasant to those about them; this rule is all the more difficult to apply because it must always be subordinated to our first rule, 'Never tell a lie.' (*Emile*, 406)

The training of women is almost solely dedicated to training a woman to be charming for the man and a virtuous mother for children. Sophie's mind is acute rather than precise, and she has an easy temperament (though variable). She knows best the tasks of her sex like dressmaking. "Sophie's mind is pleasing but not brilliant, and thorough but not deep..." (*Emile*, 429). Her mother and father taught her how to dance and sing; lace-making is her favorite activity; she does not like to cook nor get dirty gardening.

Sophie's religion is simple with few dogmas and few observances. Her devotion to God is by doing good, that is, the essential observance of her religion is her morality. The love of virtue is her ruling passion. Sophie will be the disciple of her husband, not his instructor.

When Sophie's parents talk to her about marriage it is clear that Rousseau rejects the traditional idea of an arranged marriage. Instead, he argues that the parents are really only interested in uniting two positions and two properties. It is up to the couple to decide if they are naturally suitable to one another. As Sophie's father says to her: "'There is a natural suitability, there is a suitability of established usage, and a suitability which is merely conventional. Parents should decide as to the two latters, and the children themselves should decide as to the former'" (*Emile*, 434). Sophie is instructed to find her own partner who will then be subject to the parents approval. Love prevails over property or social status.

For Emile, the choice is similar except that the Tutor picks the mate for him. The real outcome is, of course, Emile's but the tutor has carefully arranged things so that Emile meets the right woman when his heart is ready. Remember that the father gave up his rights to the child when he asked the tutor to educate him and thus it is the tutor's obligation to ensure a proper marriage. In addition, the tutor will pick a mate according to Emile's nature because they share the same nature. Emile's choice is the tutor's choice.

Emile and tutor realize that his mate is not to be found in the city. They set off walking, as it is the preferred mode of travel. Emile will never be bored with these travels, even though his heart yearns for love, because the whole world is his museum. Emile has been raised to use his experience of the world as his education and, perhaps more to the point, he has been educated to learn rather than simply educated to spout facts. Rousseau compares Emile to the wandering Telemachus from the book by the same name by Archbishop Fénelon. This book, incidently, is Sophie's favorite, in fact, she is in love with the main character. She has been disappointed by all the suitors she has met until the tutor and Emile happen to cross her path.

One obstacle to their love is their differing social classes. Sophie's parents, formerly well-off, have fallen on hard times. Emile is from the wealthy class. While Rousseau eschews social convention regarding marriages in one's own class, he nonetheless cautions against too great a class divide between the couple. Prudence tells us that extreme class difference will not make for a suitable match. The central problem, however, is not with disparity of wealth but with disparity of character. Rousseau advises Emile to disregard human institutions and instead follow nature. The two classes that matter most in finding a suitable partner are those who think and those who do not think. Sophie and Emile will be ideally suited to one another because they are products of an education true to nature.

One day, while the tutor and Emile are traveling about, they lose their way but luckily happen upon a kind peasant who gives them a hearty supper. This man also sings the praises of another family, not peasants but not wealthy either, who live near by. Emile is so taken with the story that they resolve to visit this family. The daughter in this praiseworthy family is none other than Sophie. The two young people fall almost immediately in love. Emile takes up residence in a village nearby so that he can court her and yet remain at a safe distance so as to preserve her reputation. Soon they pledge themselves to each other. Theirs is a unity of character made in accordance with reason rather than opposed to it. This, according to Rousseau, is true love.

Sophie, once betrothed, is described as commanding Emile. Emile becomes her teacher, training her singing and dancing. The first kiss is in the presence of parents and tutor and all are ecstatic. After the kiss, Sophie's mother lectures Emile. The gist of her lecture is that while it is one thing to kiss a girl on the mouth in front of her parents, it is quite another to kiss the hem of her dress in private. Emile is not to take liberty with Sophie in private. When Emile's passions seem to be at their height, the tutor warns him not to allow his passions to cloud his reason. He begins this conversation by asking Emile what he would do if informed that his beloved was dead. This is a crucial moment in the education of Emile because it is precisely the moment when virtue is understood. Virtue is truly comprehended when it conflicts with passions or, as Rousseau writes in the *Reveries*, the true test of duty is when it is contrary to inclination. The tutor explains:

> 'My son, there is no happiness without courage, nor virtue without a struggle. The word virtue is derived from a word signifying strength, and strength is the foundation of all virtue. Virtue is the heritage of a creature weak by nature but strong by will; that is the whole merit of the righteous man; and though we call God good we do not call Him virtuous, because He does good without effort. I waited to explain the meaning of this word, so often profaned, until you were ready to understand me. As long as virtue is quite easy to practice, there is little need to know it. This need arises with the awakening of the passions; your time has come.' (*Emile*, 489)

The tutor instructs Emile to learn to forsake everything if virtue requires it, even his loved one. True freedom is living according to the constraints of reason and not being subject to the fluctuations of the heart. In order to learn this lesson, the tutor instructs Emile to leave Sophie for a period of two years. The reader is not told what Sophie does during those two years, presumably she continues her education in being a good wife and mother. Emile and his tutor will travel in order to observe various governments and cultures. Emile will, in other words, learn how to be a citizen. His task is to know mankind and he must meet a number of men in order to know mankind since "...every nation has its own specific character..." (*Emile*, 497). Emile is also seeking a suitable country in which to settle his family. He will return to Sophie knowing about politics and political philosophy, the duties of citizenship, and how to represent his family in the state. In searching for Sophie, Emile was learning social relations. Now that he has found her, he must learn civil relations:

> Now after he has considered himself in his physical relations to other creatures, in his moral relations with other men, there remains to be considered his civil relations with his fellow-citizens. To do this he must first study the nature of government in general, then the different forms of government, and lastly the particular government under which he was born, to know if it suits him to live under it; for by a right which nothing can abrogate, every man, when he comes of age, becomes his own master, free to renounce the contract by which he forms part of the community, by leaving the country in which that contract holds good. It is only by sojourning in that country, after he has come to years of discretion, that he is supposed to have tacitly confirmed the pledge given by his ancestors. He acquires the right to renounce his country, just as he has the right to renounce all claim to his father's lands; yet his place of birth was a gift of nature, and in renouncing it, he renounces what is his own. Strictly speaking, every man remains in the land of his birth at his own risk unless he voluntarily submits to its laws in order to acquire a right to their protection. (*Emile*, 502)

In the midst of describing Emile's travel, Rousseau gives a brief summary of the *Social Contract* which was published the same year as *Emile*. This is only natural given that Rousseau contends that the nature of the society is discernable from the nature of the contract that formed it. Civil government arises only after the contract of society. As the *Social Contract* is the subject of the next chapter, we will return directly to the story of Emile and Sophie.

After two years of travel, Emile returns to Sophie and the two are even more certain of their love for one another. They are married with

Education

the blessings of Sophie's parents and the blessings of Emile's tutor. The tutor's work is complete though he offers the newly married couple some advice to keep their marriage strong. As with everything guiding the education of Emile, nature plays the primary role. The tutor counsels the couple to fulfill their natural roles virtuously saying to Sophie, for example, "When Emile became your husband, he became your head, it is yours to obey; this is the will of nature. When the wife is like Sophie, it is, however, good for the man to be led by her; that is another of nature's laws, and it is to give you as much authority over his heart, as his sex gives him over your person, that I have made you the arbiter of his pleasures" (*Emile,* 531; see also *Julie,* 307).

The book ends with a touching scene between former student and tutor. A few months have passed since the joyous nuptials and Emile returns to see his master. He announces that he and Sophie are expecting their first child. Rousseau knows his education has been successful when Emile says that he will educate his own child in the manner he was educated, seeking advice from his former tutor whenever necessary.[1]

Endnotes

1. Rousseau worked on a sequel to *Emile* called *Emile and Sophie, ou les Solitaires.* In the extant portion of this piece, less than fifty pages, Sophie and Emile suffer the loss of their second child and move to Paris. Emile becomes embroiled in social events and Sophie takes a lover. Her infidelity results in a pregnancy and Emile leaves her and their son for self-imposed exile.

4
Politics

As we saw in *Emile*, Rousseau was torn between describing the natural man or the citizen. This tension reappears as a tension between solitude and sociality. In short, Rousseau holds that "Men are wicked, Man is good." Individual man is born naturally good, society creates inequality and evil. This inequality results from our own devising and is most clearly seen in the inequalities of property. In *Emile*, Rousseau warns that we are on the brink of revolution because of the disparity between social classes and, in *Political Economy*, he exhorts law to protect the lower classes against the tyranny of the wealthy. Arguably, this concern is the central focus of Rousseau's political writings.

This chapter presents the two most important political pieces in Rousseau's collected works, the *Discourse on the Origin and Foundation of Inequality among Mankind* (or *Second Discourse*) and the *Social Contract*. The *Second Discourse* examines the state of nature and the evolution of moral or political inequality from this natural state. Rousseau's thorough social critique traces the sources of the limits we place on our own liberty and shows how this "enslavement" becomes cemented in law.

The *Social Contract* might be viewed as a sort of remedy for the subjugation experienced in society. Rousseau attempts to reconstruct society preserving the individual's natural goodness. He does this by creating a theoretical state in which some of the freedoms of the state of nature are sacrificed for greater freedom and happiness in civil society. Whereas the individual was isolated in the state of nature, in civil society the individual becomes part of a greater whole. A crucial difference between his social contract and the organization of society that he critiques is that his uses the natural virtue of the individual as a foundation of the state rather than supplanting that virtue with the rule of law. But as we saw in the previous chapter, individuals must be taught to be virtuous. In the state, they are virtuous insofar as their will conforms to the general will as explained further below.

Discourse on the Origin of Inequality

Rousseau dedicated the *Discourse on Inequality*, published in 1755, to the Republic of Geneva. In this dedication he falsely represents the government of Geneva as fair and just, the best form of government, a model for other nations. He uses this false flattery to win their favor. In his youth, Rousseau had exalted feelings about Geneva but by the time of the writing of the *Confessions* he recognized his idealism saying, "The noble ideal of liberty exalted my spirit, while at the same time the thought of equality, unity, and gentleness of manners moved me to tears, and inspired me with a keen regret that I had lost all those blessings. How wrong I was, and yet how natural was my mistake! I imagined that I saw all this in my native land, because I carried it in my own heart" (*Confessions*, 141).

The purpose of the *Second Discourse* "...is to point out, in the progress of things, that moment, when, right taking place of violence, nature became subject to law; to unfold that chain of amazing events, in consequence of which the strong submitted to serve the weak, and the people to purchase imaginary ease, at the expense of real happiness" (*Second Discourse*, 176). Rousseau's aim is to find out the cause of inequality among humans but in order to do so he must know the natural individual. Society, however, has hidden humans from themselves, obscuring the souls Nature gave them. Man is hardly recognizable because society has so changed him.

Using Natural Law as his basis, Rousseau traces the origin of inequality from the primitive state of natural inequalities such as differences in physical strength, age, health, and mental faculties, to the current state of moral or political inequalities sanctioned by social convention. The first principles of Natural Law pertain to self-preservation and pity; Rousseau explains these two principles or instincts, saying "...one of them interests us deeply in our own preservation and welfare, the other inspires us with a natural aversion to seeing any other begin, but especially any being like ourselves, suffer or perish" (*Second Discourse*, 171).

In searching for the cause of inequality, Rousseau posits a hypothetical state of nature. In this natural state the individual is perfectly free, independent, and solitary. Individual humans are also naturally good. Concerned only with preservation, the individual's desires are easily fulfilled through his or her own power. Saying that "most of our ills are of our own making, and that we might have avoided them all by adhering to the simple, uniform and solitary way of life prescribed to us by nature," Rousseau lists everything from idleness, to gastro-intestinal trouble as cause of our misery (*Second Discourse*, 183). In the state of nature there are few sources of illness because there is little need to commune with others, thus there is no need for doctors.

Rousseau examines the distinctions as well as the similarities between animals and humans in the state of nature. The main thing that humans have that animals do not is freedom; humans act in liberty whereas animals act on instinct. Because animals have senses, they have ideas and a sort of understanding. The other major faculty that distinguishes humans from animals is the ability to make progress.

There would be no progress if the state of nature continued because no one would work the earth, for example, if the fruits of his or her labor could be stolen from him or her. As our needs change and increase we develop passions which improve reason and brings about progress. Of course, as we begin to rely on others we begin to need a shared means of communication. Rousseau discusses the origin of language; indeed, this is an underlying theme of the entire *Second Discourse*. He temporarily closes the discussion of language by asking whether society was needed to create languages or languages to create society.

The dependency mentioned in the previous paragraph creates a sociality and also a moral life. Morals are not present in the state of nature largely because there is no social intercourse. But dependency also makes individuals weak. This claim is presented in *Emile* as well. Emile is to be educated in relative isolation so as to be strong. It is only very late in his education that the tutor introduces him to social intercourse and morality.

Although there is no morality in the state of nature, or no need for morality, there is, according to Rousseau, a natural virtue: pity. All social virtues stem from this natural virtue. "It is therefore certain that pity is a natural sentiment, which, by moderating in every individual the activity of self-love, contributes to the mutual preservation of the whole species" (*Second Discourse*, 204). Pity changes the Golden Rule to "Do good to yourself with as little prejudice as you can to others" (*Second Discourse*, 204). Pity aids social intercourse by mediating the love of self; Rousseau thus makes the sentiment whereby an individual feels the pain and suffering experienced by others the foundation of morality. Love, often thought to hold this place, is a physical impulse first and a moral aspect when tied to beauty and merit found in comparison.

Rousseau has taken us from the primitive state of nature where individuals live in isolation to a basic form of social existence beginning with the family. Inequality is hardly present and certainly little felt in the state of nature. Primitive man would remain quite simple and independent. There would be no improvement or education as there was no means of communicating any new discovery or invention. There is also no law of "mine and thine." But because his needs are simple and his passions few, the primitive man is happy:

> Let us conclude that savage man, wandering about in the forests, without industry, without speech, without any fixed residence, an equal stranger to war and every social tie, without any need of his fellows, as well as without any desire of hurting them, and perhaps even without ever distinguishing them individually one from the other, subject to few passions, and finding in himself all he wants, let us, I say, conclude that savage man had no knowledge or feelings but such as were proper to that situation; that he felt only his real necessities, took notice of nothing but what it was his interest to see, and that his understanding made as little progress as his vanity. (*Second Discourse*, 207; cf. *Emile*, 51-52)

Civil society, according to Rousseau, arises as a result of property: "The first man, who after enclosing a piece of ground, took it into his head to say, *this is mine*, and found people simple enough to believe him, was the real founder of civil society" (*Second Discourse*, 211). At first glance, there appears to be a contradiction regarding property between what is said in *Emile* and the *Second Discourse*. In the latter, Rousseau shows a clear disgust for private property but as we saw in the previous chapter, in teaching the child about morals the tutor first teaches about rights, and in particular, rights to private property. Rousseau himself notes this contradiction when he has Emile state, "I remember that my property was the origin of our inquiries. You argued very forcibly that I could not keep both my wealth and my liberty; but when you wished me to be free and at the same time without needs, you desired two incompatible things, for I could only be independent of men by returning to dependence on nature" (*Emile*, 523). Rousseau resolves the contradiction between keeping wealth and being free in the *Emile* by arguing that one must maintain a sort of detached attitude toward wealth. In *Political Economy* the resolution is to keep people from being poor; and in the *Social Contract* he advises avoiding great disparities in wealth among citizens of the state.

Rousseau continues his analysis of property in the *Second Discourse* explaining that it soon becomes burdensome because it requires more power than a single individual can provide. In other words, property weakens the individual because it makes him or her dependent on others. As difficulties arose, in their efforts to care for themselves, it became necessary for individuals to become dependent on others. At first this is through obtaining the assistance of others to reap what nature provides but soon agriculture and metallurgy bring about a revolution of sorts.

> ...as long as they undertook such works only as a single person could finish, and stuck to such arts as did not require the joint endeavors of several hands, they lived free, healthy, honest and happy, as much as their nature would admit, and continued to enjoy with each other all the pleasures of an independent intercourse; but from the moment one man began to stand in need of another's assistance; from the moment it appeared an advantage for one man to possess enough provisions for two, equality vanished; property was introduced; labor became necessary; and boundless forests became smiling fields, which had to be watered with human sweat, and in which slavery and misery were soon seen to sprout out and grow with the harvests. (*Second Discourse*, 220)

But social communion is not merely mutual assistance. Another form of being with others is through competition. In either case, the individual aims at self-preservation.

According to Rousseau, the habit of living together preceded familial love. At this point in the development of society there also occurred a gender division of labor. Prior to this family living, the occupations of the sexes were the same. Individuals lost some of their strength in defending themselves but this was made up for by the joint strength or common resistance that their union produced. Similarly, things were produced to ease the burden of subsistence yet in creating conveniences to make existence easier humans also created their first yoke. The conveniences soon became needs and the body too adapted to them.

The natural differences become more entrenched once property is introduced. The most dextrous, for instance, was the most efficient and productive with labor while the most ingenious was the best at reducing his labor to good account. Inequality results. Notice too that things are valued differently. The tool maker and the farmer may work equally hard but their products are valued differently by society. As Rousseau explains, these differences further the jealousy and create a state of opposition between individuals. "In a word, competition and rivalry on the one hand, and an opposition of interests on the other, and always a secret desire of profiting at the expense of others. Such were the first effects of property, and the inseparable attendants of nascent inequality"(*Second Discourse*, 225).

Civil law replaces natural law and cements inequality. The rich are powerful under civil law as the laws of property are primary. Various forms of government (monarchy, aristocracy, democracy) emerge because of the various or degrees of inequality in society. Most of humankind is subjected to "perpetual labor, servitude, and misery" (*Second Discourse*, 228). It should be emphasized here that the right to property is merely a human convention not a natural right. This is in contrast to Locke who argues that the right to property is a natural right stemming from an individual's right to his or her own person. Inequality so described rests on human opinion; natural inequality is interior to the individual.

> By pursuing the progress of inequality in these different revolutions, we shall discover that the establishment of laws and of the right of property was the first term of it; the institution of magistrates the second; and the third and last the changing of legal into arbitrary power; so that the different states of the rich and poor were authorized by the first epoch; those of the powerful and weak by the second; and by the third those of master and slave, which formed the last degree of inequality, and the term in which all the rest at last end, until new revolutions entirely dissolve the government, or bring it back nearer to it legal constitution. (*Second Discourse*, 238)

Rousseau has thus traced the origin of inequality to its roots in property. It is no wonder that Rousseau's work inspired the French

Revolution and influenced Karl Marx and Friedrich Engels to call for a revolution to overthrow the class divisions found within capitalism.

The Social Contract

The *Social Contract* appeared in 1762 although Rousseau began developing his ideas on this topic as early as 1743-1744. Rousseau had taken a position with the French Ambassador to Venice and his *Political Institutions* provided the seed for the later *Social Contract*. In addition, in 1754 Diderot had asked Rousseau to contribute an article on political economy to *L'Encyclopédie*. This article, published the following year, discusses the "general will" for the first time, a concept that takes a central role in *Social Contract*.

"Man was born free, and everywhere he is in chains" (*Social Contract*, 7). Rousseau begins his social contract theory with these famous words aimed at critiquing the current social order. As he argued in the *Discourse on Inequality*, property is the cause of our enslavement; it makes a slave out of servants and masters alike by yoking one to another and thereby creating a dependency that civil society will legitimize in its laws. Social order, then, is an artifice or convention. Rousseau proposes getting rid of the yoke under the same conditions that one gained it. That is, he suggests the use of the social contract to ensure freedom rather than destroy it and he sets out to illustrate how this is possible.

The earliest society and the only natural one is the family. But the natural family lasts only as long as it is necessary for the preservation of the children. If the members of the family choose to remain together after the children are no longer dependent on the parents for preservation then the union is voluntary, a convention. Family is a sort of model of political society though Rousseau is careful not to support patriarchy, or the position that the state is a larger version of the family and the power of the state is traced back to the power God granted Adam. In his article "Political Economy" for *L'Encyclopédie*, Rousseau argues against patriarchy saying the only thing the two types of power have in common are that in both family and state the "rulers" are obligated to make those subject to them happy. In *Social Contract*, he says Adam was sovereign of world only because, like Robinson Crusoe, he was the only inhabitant.

The source of authority is convention or agreement, not strength or might. Rousseau argues that there is no "right of the strongest" because obeying force is not done voluntarily but out of compulsion. Yielding to force is an act of necessity and not of will, thus there is no moral element or obligation. Only lawful authorities deserve our obedience. Further, Rousseau argues that there are no natural slaves but rather that individuals alienate their liberty only for their own advantage whereas slavery would require the individual to alienate his or her liberty for the advantage of the master. If there are slaves that appear or believe themselves to be natural it is only because their predecessors were made slaves by force and they failed to break free from the bonds of slavery. This follows from the first law of nature which is self-preservation.

Having established that true authority stems not from force but from agreement, Rousseau continues his analysis of the proper authority of government from the vantage point of the citizens of the state. It is clear, Rousseau argues, that an individual cannot alienate himself to a king for that would be making himself a slave. Since an individual is born naturally free, if that person voluntarily gives up liberty, then in effect he or she is giving up humanity. Slavery is contrary to right, still more would it be contrary to right if a person could alienate his or her children.

It might be objected that in war one essentially sacrifices personal liberty on behalf of the state and in conquest becomes the slave of the conqueror because the parent state no longer protects that individual's liberty. Rousseau responds saying that a state of war is a relation between things, states, not a relation between men.

> Men are not naturally enemies, if only for the reason that, living in their primitive independence, they have no mutual relations sufficiently durable to constitute a state of peace or a state of war. It is the relation of things and not of men which constitutes war; and since the state of war cannot arise from simple personal relations, but only from real relations, private war – war between man and man – cannot exist either in the state of nature, where there is no settled ownership, or in the social state, where everything is under the authority of the laws. (*Social Contract*, 13)

Similarly, in war, the just prince may take that which belongs to the opposing state but respects the private property and person of individuals. Since war only grants the right to that which is needed to achieve its end, it is not permissible to kill citizens of the opposing state unless they are operating as agents of that state in the person of soldiers.

Having dispensed with the supposed right to slavery and other means employed to deprive an individual of his or her rights, Rousseau prepares to discuss the convention that, in accordance with natural right, ensures the liberty of all members of a society. The main thrust from the preceding is that it is not possible for a ruler to exist prior to a nation, that is, a people cannot voluntarily subject themselves to a ruler for that would be comparable to slavery. On the contrary, Rousseau argues a society or nation must exist first and from that unity, the contract of government may be formed. That which binds people together requires unanimity at least once. Even the decision to govern according to rule by majority requires that all agree to be so governed.

The social contract that results from this unanimity arises when the state of nature comes to an end. As Rousseau explains, this point is reached when individuals can no longer ensure their own self-preservation. But since the state of nature is a state of natural goodness, Rousseau wants to create a society that will continue this goodness. He describes the goal of the social contract, saying, "To find a form of association which may defend and protect with the whole force of the community the person and property of every associate, and by means of which each, coalescing with all, may nevertheless obey only himself, and remain as free as before" (*Social Contract*, 17-18). The association Rousseau finds is one wherein each member alienates him or herself not to a single ruler but to the whole community. This total alienation of all to the community means that everyone will be equal. All rights are alienated, otherwise if people retained some rights then their rights would conflict. For example, if one member maintained his right to judge the law then his judgment would obviously (at some point) conflict with the judgment of the established society. "In short, each giving himself to all, gives himself to nobody; and as there is not one associate over whom we do not acquire the same rights which we concede to him over ourselves, we gain the equivalent of all that we lose, and more power to preserve what we have" (*Social Contract*, 18).

Once the contract is in place, it cannot be changed without dissolution. We submit ourselves equally to the general will: "Each of us puts in common his person and his whole power under the supreme direction of the general will; and in return we receive every member as an indivisible part of the whole" (*Social Contract*, 18-19).

In the social contract, individuals are transformed into a moral and collective body, or what Rousseau calls the body politic (this replaces "city"). The body politic is considered a *State* by it members when it is passive; *Sovereign* when active; and *Power* when it is compared to other similar republics. Individual associates in the social contract are referred to as *people* when described collectively; *citizens* when described individually as participants in the sovereign power; and *subjects* when accountable to the laws of the State.

The move from the state of nature to civil society is a move in the individual from instinct to justice; in civil society the individual consults reason and acts on duty. Perhaps even more profound is the change to liberty. In the state of nature, liberty was ensured by the power of the individual. In the body politic, the liberty of the individual is bounded only by the general will, thereby bringing about a greater form of liberty.

> What man loses by the social contract is his natural liberty and an unlimited right to anything which tempts him and which he is able to attain; what he gains is civil liberty and property in all that he possesses. In order that we may not be mistaken about these compensations, we must clearly distinguish natural liberty, which is limited only by the powers of the individual, from civil liberty, which is limited by the general will; and possession, which is nothing but the result of force or the rights of first occupancy, from property, which can be based only on a positive title. Besides the preceding, we might add to the acquisitions of the civil state moral freedom, which alone renders man truly master of himself; for the impulse of mere appetite is slavery, while obedience to a self-prescribed law is liberty. (*Social Contract*, 23)

Whereas individuals in the state of nature were physically unequal, with the social contract each becomes equal to all others under the law.

In joining the social contract, the individual alienates his property as well as his person to the community. Rousseau argues that the State becomes owner of all individuals' property by the social contract. Ownership of property by the State does not mean that the individual loses all rights to property. On the contrary, it is precisely in giving up his or her property that the individual is secured in his or her property. Recall that in the state of nature there was no right to property but merely right to possession ensured merely by personal strength. With the establishment of civil society, the real right to property is established. The State legalizes the right to first occupancy insofar as certain conditions hold. An individual may legally acquire only enough property as is needed for subsistence through his or her labor insofar as the land

Politics

is not previously occupied by someone else. Each person has a right to what he or she needs but does not have a right to the excess.

Notice from the clarification of names above that the *Sovereign* is not a ruler with whom the people contract but is the collective of all of the people themselves. Each individual is in the double relation "as a member of the Sovereign towards individuals, and as a member of the State towards the Sovereign" (*Social Contract*, 20). Rousseau further specifies the role of the Sovereign. The active body politic can never create a law it cannot break nor can it ever impose a law on itself that would contradict the original contract. To change the original contract, whether by submitting to another power or by breaking off a portion of the body politic, is to dissolve the original social contract. Further, since the Sovereign is constituted by the individuals who created it, it follows that one member cannot be harmed without harming the entire body politic. This clearly lends itself to individual members of the state faithfully aiding each other. Rousseau calls the will of the Sovereign, that is the will of the people, the *general will*. If a citizen regarded his own particular will as more important than the general will then he or she might be inclined to skirt their duties. To avoid this, Rousseau says that "whoever refuses to obey the general will shall be constrained to do so by the whole body; which means nothing else than that he shall be forced to be free" (*Social Contract*, 22).

The general will is perhaps the most difficult concept in all of Rousseau's work. Some commentators appeal to this concept of the general will as evidence of Rousseau's totalitarianism. Others use it to illustrate his indebtedness to the natural law tradition. Still others hold up Rousseau as a model of the classical liberal. Regardless, it is clear that according to Rousseau it is the general will alone that directs the state to the common good, which makes society possible in the first place. While the general will is often decided by a majority vote, it is not the case that the majority opinion is the general will. Their common interest not the number of votes unites a people. Rousseau is also quite explicit that no one be excluded from the vote.

Establishing an absolute authority or a master is the same as destroying the body politic as the Sovereign no longer exists. This would be comparable to an individual abdicating his or her liberty; both are examples of slavery. The magistrates nonetheless have the power to make decisions for the people. Such decisions are statements of the general will or accord with it insofar as the people as Sovereign do not oppose the decisions. Silence on their part indicates that the magistrate's acts are not contrary to the general will.

From the foregoing, one can discern that the statement of the general will is the law of the state. It also follows, then, that the law must be the will of the entire Sovereign body and not merely the will of a portion of it. Nor is the statement of the general will to be confused with applications of law such as the declaration of war or resolution of peace.

While the general will cannot be mistaken because it is not possible for people to desire what is contrary to their good, the people do not always accurately apprehend their own good. There is also the risk of confusing the will of all of the members of the body politic with the general will. Rousseau offers the following formula for distinguishing the general will from the will of all: "There is often a great deal of difference between the will of all and the general will; the latter regards only the common interest, while the former has regard to private interests and is merely a sum of particular wills; but take away from these same wills the pluses and minuses which cancel one another, and the general will remains as the sum of differences" (*Social Contract*, 30-31).

Rousseau's aim is to ensure the greatest amount of freedom within the social contract or to preserve the benefits of the state of nature while dispensing with the problems. To avoid an unjust and inequitable society, he proposes a sort of radical democracy. As he explain, "It is important, then, in order to have a clear declaration of the general will, that there should be no partial association in the State, and that every citizen should express only his own opinion" (*Social Contract*, 31).

The social contract gives the body politic absolute power over its members. But every member equally submits so no part of the community is disadvantaged. The next task is to determine the rights of the citizen and the rights of the Sovereign. Although early in the *Social Contract* Rousseau claimed that each person alienated all his property, liberty, and person, he clarifies his position further by claiming that it is only that which is necessary to the community, or Sovereign, of which the individual is a member. Rousseau states, "It is admitted that whatever part of his power, property, and liberty each one alienates by the social compact is only that part of the whole of which the use is important to the community; but we must also admit that the Sovereign alone is judge of what is important" (*Social Contract*, 32-33).

Justice follows from equality; the general will must come from each in order to be applicable to all. The general will cannot decide on particular matters or have a particular end, it would no longer be general. "[T]he social compact establishes among the citizens such an equality that they all pledge themselves under the same conditions and ought all to enjoy the same rights" (*Social Contract*, 34). An act of sovereignty is an agreement with each of its members, not an agreement between people and magistrate. Thus people obey no one but their own will. Subjects submit to that which is for they best welfare and to which they have agreed. What is more, an act of sovereignty, as a lawful agreement founded on the social contract, has the common good as its aim.

Two obvious questions that flow from this pertain to war and punishing criminals. If every member of the state submits equally to every other member, and if the end of the social contract is the preservation of its members for the common good, then how can some members be required to come to the aid of the state in war? Rousseau answers that there is a natural right to self-defense, that is, "Every man has a right to risk his life in order to preserve it" (*Social Contract*, 36). Since preserving one's live in the social contract is living securely in civil society, it may be necessary to give up one's life in order to do so. Acting as a soldier for the State during war is acting in self-defense.

Capital punishment is justified along similar lines: "it is in order not to be the victim of an assassin that a man consents to die if he becomes one" (*Social Contract*, 37). Anyone who violate his rights or the rights of others becomes a criminal or traitor to the social contract; he can no longer be counted a member of the state. In this state of war between the state and the criminal (or enemy of the state), either the state or the guilty person must perish. It should be remembered here that the Sovereign confers the right to condemn criminals, it does not exercise it itself for doing so is a particular act rather than a statement of the general will. The Sovereign does, however, have the sole right to pardon the criminal. Given that the criminal declares war on all the people it must be all the people, acting as Sovereign, who issue the pardon. Rousseau also notes that it is the rare individual who is incapable of being made good and thus capital punishment should not be exercised often; a state that is forced into killing criminals frequently is a weak government.

Justice is determined by nature and thus comes from God but since there is no clear executor for nature except God, it is necessary for social conventions and laws to outline the rights and duties of citizens. A law is only properly a law when it is decreed by the entire people and concerns everyone. In this way, the law is general like the general will and can never pertain to a particular action or individual. While it might set up classes of people, it cannot specify who will occupy those classes. Thus the republic is established.

Politics

Although the general will is always right, Rousseau indicates that the people may not always clearly discern it and thus a legislator is needed to guide the people in their right use of reason to determine the general will. However, the people never give up legislative power, the legislator merely acts like a god on behalf of the people in devising the institutions and laws to govern

Rousseau also considers the people of the just republic. The best constituted state would be limited in size such that it is big enough to sustain itself but small enough to be governed. If there are many cities or regions of a state then administering the laws will become difficult and paying for the various offices will become unduly burdensome on the people. So too, differences in cultures and climates make it almost impossible to share the same form of government. In his political writings, Rousseau always had in mind a model of the city-state. In addition, the people must be good and capable of following the law.

> What nation, then, is adapted for legislation? That which is already united by some bond of interest, origin, or convention, but has not yet borne the real yoke of the laws; that which has neither customs nor superstitions firmly rooted; that which has no fear of being overwhelmed by sudden invasion, but which, without entering into the disputes of its neighbors, can singlehanded resist either of them, or aid one in repelling the other, that in which every member can be known by all, and in which there is no necessity to lay on a man a greater burden than a man can bear; that which can subsist without other nations, and without which every other nation can subsist, that which is neither rich nor poor and is self-sufficing; lastly, that which combines the stability of an old nation with the docility of a new one. (*Social Contract*, 53-54)

A system of legislation, having the common good as its primary interest, ought to have the goals of liberty and equality. Rousseau defends liberty as a principle goal of legislation because the opposite of liberty weakens the entire state. Equality means that no one should be forced to submit to another by violence or coercion; it does not mean equality in property though Rousseau does think that the just state will not have anyone who is too rich or too poor. These general goals of liberty and equality are modified according to the inhabitants and the location of the State. Each State, then, has a government that is best adapted to its conditions; the best state is that which is best for a particular people in a particular area.

Rousseau divides law into four classifications: political law, civil law, criminal law, and customs or opinion. Civil law pertains to citizens' interactions with each other while criminal law pertains to the individual citizen who disobeys the law. Public opinion and customs have the force of law but are not written as part of legislation. Finally, political law which determines the institutions of the state, or the relation between the people as Sovereign and the people as State, determines the specifics of government for the republic. As the Sovereign, all of the people are required to enact a law but may use representatives to execute the law.

Rousseau begins his discussion of the various forms of government by first defining government: "An intermediate body established between the subjects and the Sovereign for their mutual correspondence, charged with the execution of the laws and with the maintenance of liberty both civil and political" (*Social Contract*, 60). Government is not formed by contract as governors are commissioned and the people cannot alienate their sovereignty. The three powers of the state at this point are the legislative, the executive, and the subjects.

To determine the form of government best suited to a state, Rousseau offers as a rule that the government should be stronger if the population is large so as to ensure that law is more powerful than custom. But since the government is a tool of the Sovereign, the governors ought to always use the general will as their will. Otherwise, if particular wills are used in government, the body politic is dissolved.

Rousseau identifies three basic forms of government: democracy, aristocracy, and monarchy. The entire population is responsible for government in a democracy, whereas an aristocracy has many more ordinary citizens than governors and a monarchy places the executive power in the hands of a single person. The general rule is that "democratic government is suitable to small States, aristocracy to those of moderate size, and monarchy to large ones" (*Social Contract*, 69).

Democracy, according to Rousseau, is probably not suitable for most states because it requires that the people never let their particular wills interfere with their obligation to the general will. Nonetheless, it does seem fitting that those who make the laws ought to execute them. In the end, Rousseau holds that democracy requires a small state to allow for the assembly of the people, relative equality in wealth, and simple customs. The difficulty of combining all these characteristics, which are the same characteristics Rousseau used to describe the perfect State, make it nearly impossible to imagine a pure democracy.

Aristocracy may be either hereditary, elective, or natural. Natural aristocracy is rarely seen as it is rather close to the primitive society. Hereditary aristocracy is, according to Rousseau, the worst form of government as it made power a result of inheritance. Elective aristocracy is the best form of government in part because it gives a choice to the people and because it allows the magistrates to meet frequently. Elective aristocracy is supposed to be the rule by the wisest, who may correspond to the wealthiest, but Rousseau also cites the benefit of occasionally electing someone from the lower social ranks to show that merit is more important than wealth.

Monarchy, with its single magistrate, is well suited to large, wealthy states but is also a dangerous form of government because the particular will of the monarch easily usurps the general will of the state. Rousseau includes a scathing critique of absolute monarchy noting that it is extremely rare that a person of merit occupies that office. A hereditary monarchy adds the additional problem of occasionally ceding the throne to a child. Rousseau had no doubt understood the consequences of this when Louis the XIV died in France and the country spent eight years in regency until Louis XV assumed office in 1723. This critique raised the ire of the King but also contributed to the fomenting unrest among the common people that would eventually lead to the French Revolution.

In general, the mark of a good government is prosperity. But governments also seem to degenerate naturally according to Rousseau. For instance, inevitably the governors change the constitution thereby oppressing the people as Sovereign. Rousseau further identifies two ways the government deteriorates: when government contracts by passing from democracy to aristocracy or aristocracy to monarchy, or when the State itself is dissolved either by the governor(s) acting outside the law or by assuming the sovereign power (for example, if the King forbid the assembly of the sovereign people). If the State is dissolved, then the social contract is void and people are thrust back into a state of nature.

Thus government is instituted when the Sovereign (that is the people) determine that a governing body is needed and what form it will take. This is an act of law. Next, the people elect those who will fill the role of governors in the established system. This act is not a law because it pertains to particular individuals and actions.

Once the government is in place, the next question is how to ensure that the general will is the force and end of the State's actions. Recall that the general will is constant but that humans, individually or collectively, may be mistaken in their determination of the general will. Rousseau offers the majority vote as the clearest indication of the general will. The vote of the majority, after the social contract has been established, binds all members of the state. The person who voted contrary to the majority was simply mistaken in his or her understanding of the general will.

> The citizen consents to all the laws, even to those which are passed in spite of him, and even to those which punish him when he dares to violate any of them. The unvarying will of all the members of the State is the general will; it is through that that they are citizens and free. When a law is proposed in the assembly of the people, what is asked of them is not exactly whether they approve the proposition or reject it, but whether it is conformable or not to the general will, which is their own; each one in giving his vote expresses his opinion thereupon; and from the counting of the votes is obtained the declaration of the general will. (*Social Contract*, 113)

For serious matters, such as laws, the majority vote should be close to unanimous. For less serious matters, such as particular applications of law, the majority vote may vary from the minority by as little as one vote.

All that remains for governing a just state is a discussion of public opinion and civil religion. Rousseau argues in favor of censorship although the bulk of the argument is found in his *Letter to M. D'Alembert*. Censorship is useful for preserving morality by keeping opinions free of corruption. It plays an analogous role to law: "Just as the declaration of the general will is made by law, the declaration of public opinion is made by the censorship" (*Social Contract*, 134).

Rousseau's position regarding civil religion, like his *Profession of Faith of a Savoyard Vicar*, calls for religious tolerance which is inseparable from civil tolerance. As for the specifics of faith in relation to the State, Rousseau sums up his position in the following quotation:

> Now it is very important for the State that every citizen should have a religion which may make him delight in his duties; but the dogmas of this religion concern neither the State nor its members, except so far as they affect morality and the duties which he who professes it is bound to perform towards others. (*Social Contract*, 145)

Thus the State is constituted so as to retain the natural goodness of human individuals.

5
Arts and Letters

Rousseau's influence on art and literature was nothing short of immense. He marked the beginning of Romanticism and influenced scores of philosophers, writers, artists, and even scientists. This chapter summarizes some of his essays, focusing on the *Discourse on the Sciences and Arts* and the *Letter to M. D'Alembert on the Theater,* then examines his novel *Julie, ou La Nouvelle Héloïse*. Both of the essays demonstrate Rousseau's position on nature and inequality; the novel does this as well but also illustrates the "beautiful soul" which, rather than imitating nature with social propriety, simply or naturally exudes virtue. The *Discourse on the Sciences and Arts* is Rousseau's first major work. It won the Academy of Dijon prize in 1750 and was published in 1751. In this short piece one can discern much of Rousseau's thought; he emphasizes virtue and truth over public opinion and he rejects social and economic inequalities.

First Discourse

While walking to Vincennes to visit Diderot who was imprisoned there, Rousseau read the subject for an essay contest by the Academy of Dijon. The theme was "Whether the Restorations of the Sciences and Arts has contributed to the purification of morals." He entered the contest and won. Ironically, the first two winners were the only essays to answer negatively. His essay, published as *Discourse on the Sciences and Arts*, often referred to as the *First Discourse*, argues against Enlightenment progress in the arts and sciences and blames such progress for the corruption of morals in contemporary society. "Here is how I would arrange that genealogy. The first source of evil is inequality; from inequality arose riches; for the words poor and rich are relative, and wherever men are equal there is neither rich nor poor. From riches are born luxury and idleness; from luxury arose the fine Arts, and from idleness the Sciences" (*First Discourse, Replies*, 45). Modern progress in the arts and sciences fails to teach morality.

Rousseau begins by arguing that the cultivation of knowledge creates needs and desires which, as we saw in the discussion of the *Second Discourse*, gives rise to a sort of enslavement to civilized tastes. Morals and character become propriety and public opinion. The irony, of course, is that in progressing we actually digress in that we obscure truth and virtue with the false manners of society: "...our souls have been corrupted in proportion to the advancement of our Sciences and Arts to perfection" (*First Discourse*, 7). Next, Rousseau offers a brief survey of historical progress and the evils it brought with it to places like Rome, Egypt, Greece and Constantinople. Modern China is held up as an example of the inverse relation between the development of the Arts and the depravity of the people. In contrast, Persia, Germany, and of course, Sparta, demonstrate a love of virtue instead of a false attention to tastes.

Using Socrates' argument in Plato's *Republic* that the poets and the artists propagate a false knowledge, Rousseau argues that the proliferation of knowledge is not beneficial to humankind. Instead, it simply teaches us more falsehoods; to paraphrase what Rousseau says, when we begin to study virtue we forget how to practice it (*First Discourse*, 11). Using courage as an example, he shows how the idleness of study diminishes the strength of the body and weakens the will.

In the second half of the *First Discourse*, Rousseau addresses the Arts and the Sciences directly. He notes that their aims are futile and their influence corrupting. "Born in idleness, they nourish it in turn; and irreparable loss of time is the first injury they necessarily cause society" (*First Discourse*, 13). What is more, the knowledge that is being spread plants doubt in the hearts of the people. They begin to question faith and politics. Notice that this seems contradictory to Rousseau's thought. A proponent of democracy and opponent of public opinion ought not to suggest that the people fail to question political authority and scorn public opinion. Indeed this contradiction is troublesome but Rousseau's fear is that in questioning faith and politics the people will abandon all virtue, even the prejudices of society, rather than seek true virtue. After all, it is the rare individual who will succeed in understanding virtue. His other worry is that those brilliant men (for they are men according to Rousseau) who do esteem virtue will be encouraged to lower themselves to the level of public decorum thereby failing to attain the knowledge of which they are truly capable.

Rousseau concludes his essay noting the wisdom of the so-called Philosophers (citing Spinoza and Hobbes specifically but indicating many others). Each one thinks he knows the truth but their teachings merely contradict one another. He further blames the ease with which books are printed and distributed with disseminating the sciences and arts and thus spreading the corruption of morals.

The essay ends with a plea for people to do their duty. Rousseau offers a Platonic account of individuals' duties saying that very few will be endowed by nature to study the Sciences and Arts and discern the true laws of nature. Most of us are better off pursuing what nature intended for us than trying in vain to obtain knowledge. Happiness is found not in public opinion but in fulfilling our individual talents.

On the Theater

Rousseau continues these comments on the impact of the Arts and Sciences on morality in the *Preface to Narcissus: Or the Lover of Himself* written in 1752 for publication early in 1753. In this preface, he defends and reiterates his position and makes clear that it is a system he articulates and not just a response to the Dijon Academy's question.

In his defense of the *First Discourse* he says "I showed that the source of our errors on this point comes from the fact that we mistake our vain and deceitful knowledge for the sovereign intelligence which sees the truth of everything at a glance" (*Preface to Narcissus*, 190-191). Taste eclipsing morality results from idleness and the desire to make oneself unique. But, argues Rousseau, if a State is well constituted and governed then each citizen is equal to every other and all have their specific duties. There is no desire to mark oneself off as different or better than the rest. In other words, Rousseau foreshadows his *Discourse on Inequality* and *Social Contract* by claiming that individuals are naturally good but that poor government and corrupt society enslave them to their passions.

Rousseau is practical in his criticism. He says that the Sciences and Arts are responsible for making good people bad but he also says that once that transition is made it is important to keep the Sciences and Arts ("Academies, Colleges, Universities, Libraries, Theatres") as a means of diverting corrupt individuals from pursuing their wickedness with other things (*Preface to Narcissus*, 196).

This preface to Rousseau's short play *Narcissus* does not attempt to explain or justify his play. The play was written when Rousseau was quite young (he says 18 in the *Preface* but corrects it in the *Confessions* by adding a few years). *Narcissus* is an amusing comedy about a young groom, Valentine, who falls in love with a feminized picture of himself hours before he is to be married. After searching in vain all over Paris for this "charming object," Valentine foolishly seeks to postpone his wedding so that he might have a greater chance of pursuing his new love. Eventually the ruse is made known and Valentine must seek the forgiveness of his betrothed: "Well, my fair Angelica; you have cured me of a foible, which was the disgrace of my youth: and for the future I hope to experience in your society, that when we truly love another, we cease to be fond of ourselves" (*Narcissus*, 29). It was staged on 18 December 1752 by the Comédie-Française and Rousseau was so bored that he soon canceled the production.

Although he wrote for the theater, even composing a comic opera, *Le Devin du Village* (*The Village Soothsayer*), Rousseau reminds his reader that he writes not for praises or glory but to make individuals good. His work is to inspire those who read it to do good; if it fails in this regard it is because only a very few can understand his message.

Barring this nurturing of virtue, the theater has one other advantage which Rousseau mentions in *Emile*. Rousseau recommends taking Emile to the theater in order to study taste: "I take him to the theatre to study taste, not morals; for in the theatre above all taste is revealed to those who can think" (*Emile*, 369). Rousseau's most complete analysis of the theater occurs in his *Letter to M. D'Alembert on the Theatre*. Rousseau responds to an article D'Alembert had written for *L'Encyclopédie* on Geneva. Among other things, D'Alembert had argued that Geneva ought to have a theater. Certainly such a theater would be beneficial to Voltaire and Diderot but Rousseau found the suggestion quite offensive for his birthplace. In the *Republic*, Plato condemns the Poets who claim to be wise but are not. In the *First Discourse,* Rousseau uses this passage from the *Republic* to support his argument that the Arts obscure truth and virtue. Here in the *Letter to D'Alembert,* Rousseau continues Plato's position by arguing for censorship of the dramatic arts.

Rousseau makes two main points in his argument against the theater and in defense of Geneva. First, he focuses on the theater's impact on public and private morality. The need for theatrical entertainment arises because of idleness, while hard work is its own amusement.

> The good use of time makes time even more precious, and the better one puts it to use, the less one can find to lose. Thus it is constantly seen that the habit of work renders inactivity intolerable and that a good conscience extinguishes the taste for frivolous pleasure. But it is discontent with one's self, the burden of idleness, the neglect of simple and natural tastes that makes foreign amusement so necessary. (*Letter to D'Alembert*, 16)

Rousseau further analyzes both comedy and tragedy and finds that their form of imitation, rather than leading to the perfection of virtue, praises vice. The virtuous man becomes the target of humor while the wicked man triumphs or earns the pity of the audience. These dramas encourage viewers to allow passions to rule reason rather than the other way around. More importantly, they confuse the passions through imitation. Viewers feel pity for the villain and love for the reprobate. By way of example, Rousseau offers a lengthy criticism of Molière's *Misanthrope*. This is often cited as the first such example of literary criticism. Misdirecting passion in the theater leads to misplaced feelings in real life. "The harm for which the theatre is reproached is not precisely that of inspiring criminal passions but of disposing the soul to feelings which are too tender and which are later satisfied at the expense of virtue" (*Letter to D'Alembert*, 51).

Morality is also endangered by introducing actors and actresses into society. In Rousseau's day, these professionals were reputed to have loose lifestyles and corrupt morals. Their presence would surely adversely influence others in society.

The second approach to his argument might be called the approach from political economy. As in *Political Economy* and *Emile*, Rousseau argues that certain of the arts foment luxury which merely furthers the inequality among peoples. In the *Letter to D'Alembert*, Rousseau focuses on the economic impact a theater would have on Geneva. He traces the origins of five disadvantages. The first is a "slackening of work" as people will be encouraged to pursue amusement rather than work. They might leave work early in order to attend the theater or they might consume valuable work time thinking or talking about the plays (*Letter to D'Alembert*, 62-63).

The second disadvantage, "increase of expenses," stems from the first. Work clothes would be unsuitable for a theater performance so individuals will be forced to spend more on clothes and other newly created needs. Next, Rousseau argues there will be a "decrease in trade" because less is produced and thus prices are higher. Former trading partners will abandon Geneva in search of lower prices among more industrious peoples. The fourth disadvantage is the "establishment of taxes." Taxes are needed in order to pave roads and keep them passable in the winter so that people may attend the theater.

The last disadvantage is the "introduction of luxury." Rousseau argues that women will attend the theater not just to see the show but to be seen as well. Those with different social statuses will want to demonstrate their status with their dress. Rousseau uses the example of the wife of a magistrate and the wife of a schoolmaster. Since the former wants to be distinguished from the latter, and the latter wants to be adorned like the former, numerous inequalities and economic hardships will result (*Letter to D'Alembert*, 63).

Before moving on to his proposal for an alternate form of entertainment, one which foster morals rather than subverts them, Rousseau fortifies his position by arguing that the theater makes men into women. Men would be forced into adopting the preferences and virtues of women. They would become softened, both physically and mentally, by the disadvantages of the dramatic arts described above.

The *Letter to D'Alembert* concludes with a proposal for what Rousseau believes to be appropriate amusements for Geneva. In essence, his suggestion is a sort of public dance that would allow the intermingling of the sexes under the watchful eyes of parents. Rather than misdirect the passions, this sort of entertainment would foster morality by bringing out the different virtues of the sexes. It would also serve the useful purpose of exercising the body whereas theater contributes to idleness. In addition, young men and women will have the benefit of courting each other and deciding for themselves who to marry. Thus love, rather than the false proprieties, wins the day. This theme of balancing the passions and virtue is also the framework of Rousseau's novel to which we now turn.

Julie, ou La Nouvelle Héloïse

Rousseau's novel is most commonly known simply as *La Nouvelle Héloïse*[1] but this was in fact not the title that Rousseau usually used in referring to it. He usually called it by the simple name of *Julie* and insisted that the first title page of the published edition read *Julie ou La Nouvelle Héloïse*. The second title page contained the additional title *Letter of Two Lovers Who Live in a Small Town at the Foot of the Alps* (*Lettres de deux amans, habitans d'une petite ville au pied des Alpes*). This latter title is more descriptive in that the book is indeed an exchange of letters between two lovers and their close friends. In the first preface to *Julie, ou La Nouvelle Héloïse*, Rousseau claims he is merely the editor of the collection of letters that follows and in the second preface he argues with an imaginary "man of letters" that it does not really matter if the book be a true exchange or a creation of Rousseau. Like most of Rousseau's written work, his aim was to write a book that "lead[s] its readers to do good" (*Julie*, 214). In the *Confessions,* Rousseau records his own desire for an orchard on the shore of Lake Geneva, "a constant friend, a charming wife, a cow, and a little boat" (*Confessions*, 148). He also desired the experience of true love. He created such a life for himself in the novel and used Vevay, town on the shore of Lake Geneva, as a setting for *Julie*. But more importantly, he created two lovers who ultimately love virtue more than anything else. This love of virtue, subjecting the passions to reason, makes the two lovers unusual characters among their contemporaries who value propriety and social standing above true virtue. Rousseau says the book is "not meant to circulate in society, and is suitable for very few readers" (*Julie*, 3). Only those who believe in virtue will be moved by these passionate letters.

With the opening letter, Julie d'Étange's tutor, who remains nameless for much of the first half of the book, declares his love for her. The two are quite obviously from different social classes and their union would never be allowed by Julie's family. She is the only daughter of Baron d'Étange and is expected to marry the man her father arranges for her. Julie responds to her tutor with some short notes indicating he need not leave his position but she acts quite coldly to him during both private lessons and public events. Finally, Julie explains the reason for her chilly demeanor: she loves her tutor as much as he loves her but she knows her duty is elsewhere. This classic conflict between duty and passion frames the novel. Although duty eventually wins the day, passion fights a tough battle as both Julie and her tutor, St. Preux, grapple with their desire to be together knowing it can never be.

After declaring their mutual affections, Julie and her tutor exchange tender letters that give evidence of her beautiful soul and his burning passion. Eventually, of course, their affections are no longer expressed in the purity of letters. But they are protected by the watchful and loving eye of Julie's cousin Claire. When, in the presence of Claire, Julie kisses St. Preux for the first time, he is thrown into a state of ecstasy mingled with turmoil. In his letter describing his state he says:

> What have you done, my Julie? You meant to reward me and you have undone me. I am drunk, or rather insane. My senses are impaired, all my faculties are deranged by that fatal kiss. You meant to alleviate my sufferings? Cruel woman, you make them sharper. It is poison I have culled from your lips; it festers, it sets my blood afire, it kills me, and your pity is the death of me. (*Julie*, 51)

Julie too was affected for she fainted shortly after their lips touched. Her letter in response to St. Preux's transports, however, coldly sends him away. Although she sends her heart with him, it is clear that in the conflict of passion and duty, Julie is trying to take the side of duty.

St. Preux does go away and Julie's father returns. He is quite pleased with the education his daughter has received. He also brought with him a Monsieur de Wolmar with the intention of making this dear friend his son-in-law. When Julie and her mother were informed of this arrangement, Mme d'Étange tried to convince her husband that the good qualities St. Preux had outweighed the fact that he was not born into the right social class. The Baron d'Étange had made up his mind however. From his abode far from her, St. Preux suggests they go away together: "Come, O my soul, into your friend's arms and reunite the two halves of our being: come and in the face of heaven, guide in our flight and witness to our vows, swear we will live and die for each other" (*Julie*, 76). He ends the letter with an ominous threat that he is in such despair that he might throw himself off the cliff near his residence.

With the weight of all these feelings, Julie became gravely ill and her cousin entreats St. Preux to return to Julie's side. Claire, unfortunately, is called away and without her watchful presence the two lovers consummate their union. Julie, knowing that her father might kill her if he finds out, hopes that their first tryst will result in a pregnancy. The lovers attempt to arrange subsequent meetings and finally succeed in plotting a rendevous in Julie's room one night. St. Preux, finding a pen and paper in her wardrobe, wrote of his excitement while waiting for her presence. Alas, when her father finds out about her love for the tutor and her mother's complicity he flies into a rage beating both mother and daughter. The fall Julie suffered as part of this encounter caused her to miscarry. Her father, steeped in regret, apologizes in a very tender way to his daughter but also forbids her to see St. Preux again.

Claire's father, meanwhile, has arranged a match for her to Monsieur d'Orbe but her love for Julie requires her to wait until the latter is at peace before she can wed. Monsieur d'Orbe and another family friend, Milord Edward Bomston, arrange to take Julie's lover away and stay with him until he is out of despair. Milord Edward, an Englishman, even offered to give the two lovers some property he owns in Yorkshire but Julie's prudence, with Claire's counsel, forces her to refuse the offer and remain true to her duty. Julie is the model of a woman who was conquered before marriage but regains her virtue. Morality and marital fidelity are at the root of all social order (*Confessions*, 405).

After almost three years of being away, M. de Wolmar returns. Julie has asked her lover for his permission or rather for "her freedom" and he has granted it. His despair reaches such a peak that he contemplates suicide and it is only at the interventions of Milord Edward that he is spared. St. Preux, at Milord Edward's advice, undertakes the active life and sails around the world. Claire has married and soon has a daughter; she is also shortly widowed. Julie marries and has two sons. She has dedicated herself to marital fidelity. Her husband, many years her senior, admires her beautiful soul and the two live a very contented life.

Many years go by before the two former lovers meet again. When St. Preux writes Claire, now Mme d'Orbe, that he is coming for a visit M. and Mme de Wolmar open their house to him as well. M. de Wolmar is presented as a generous, virtuous atheist. His unbelief causes Julie some grief but she recognizes the quality of his soul. After a brief test of his wife's virtue, M. de Wolmar decides to ask St. Preux to educate his sons. St. Preux and Milord Edward travel to Rome to settle some romantic business of Milord Edward's and while traveling St. Preux learns of M. de Wolmar's intentions. He joyfully accepts the trust M. de Wolmar displays and looks forward to returning with Milord Edward to educate the children of such a happy household.

While in Rome, St. Preux receives news of Julie's death. During a family outing on a lake, Julie saw one of her children slip into the water. With a mother's love, she dove in to save him but nearly drowned herself in the process. The family returned home and she was very ill with fever. Her last moments are recorded in a letter from M. de Wolmar to St. Preux. He describes Julie's death as unlike any other. Julie's dying confession of faith avows the use of God given reason to guide behavior and dedicates life to truth; she also rejects any notion of eternal damnation. In short, Julie's statement of faith foreshadowed the *Profession of Faith of a Savoyard Vicar*. More importantly for the novel is that Julie's words and life inspired M. de Wolmar to give up his unbelief. To her, faith was a faith of the living whereas Christianity often appeared to be a faith for the dying. She died content because she had lived a virtuous life for truth.

The models for Julie d'Étange and her cousin Claire, later Mme d'Orbe, were two friends with whom Rousseau shared a delightful afternoon in his youth, Mlle Galley and Mlle de Graffenried. He had been out walking when they approached on horseback. Their horses would not cross a stream and Rousseau gallantly offered to help. After successfully leading the horses across, the two young women urged Rousseau to join them. They spent the day at the Château de la Tour and ate a picnic dinner. Rousseau even stole a kiss of Mlle Galley's hand. He was intoxicated by the two and obviously inspired by their friendship as well (*Confessions*, 132-135). He was himself the model for St. Preux:

> I imagined love and friendship, the two idols of my heart, in the most ravishing of forms, and took delight in adorning them with all the charms of the sex I had always adored. I imagined two women friends, rather than two of my own sex, since although examples of such friendships are rarer they are also more beautiful. I endowed them with analogous but different characters; with features if not perfect yet to my taste, and radiant with kindliness and sensibility. I made one dark, the other fair; one lively, the other gentle; one sensible, the other weak, but so touching in her weakness that virtue itself seemed to gain by it. I gave one of them a lover to whom the other was a tender friend and even something more; but I allowed of no rivalry or quarrels or jealousy because I find it hard to imagine any painful feelings, and I did not wish to discolor my charming picture with anything degrading to Nature. Being captivated by my two charming models, I identified myself as far as I could with the lover and friend. But I made him young and pleasant, whilst endowing him also with the virtues and faults that I felt in myself. (Confessions, 400-401)

In addition, *Julie* is replete with philosophical details. For instance, Rousseau gives us the picture of the virtuous atheist in the person of M. de Wolmar. This portrait directly challenged the beliefs of his day and was, in part, his own contribution to the debate between the irreligious *philosophes* and the Catholic Church.

Rousseau also discusses the different natures of the sexes and argues that, in education, example is superior to rules. Clearly, *Julie*, which was finished four years before *Emile*, set the foundation for the latter. Julie is quite explicit both in her letters to St. Preux and in her dying remarks reported by M. de Wolmar that girls ought not to be educated in the same manner as boys. The two sexes are so entirely different (*Julie*, 104, 370-372). Rousseau was opposing many of his contemporaries with these remarks. While others argued for more equality in education for females, he held up domestic life as the true nature of women. Nonetheless, he did not think women should have all things decided for them. On the contrary, as both *Julie* and *Emile* demonstrate, Rousseau was not in favor of arranged marriages. He favored a union of love over a union of estates and thought the couple themselves should decide whether to marry.

Another important aspect of *Julie* is its setting. The novel is set in a small country village rather than a large city. Once again Rousseau countered his contemporaries by making the subtle claim that what goes on in the city is pretense while the provinces offer the openness for virtue and truth to prevail. In the city, individuals are constantly subject to public opinion and judge their behavior by fickle prejudice. But among family in the country-side, individuals are free to live a simple life in accordance with truth. Indeed, throughout *Julie* Rousseau incorporated subtle social criticism and advanced his own ideas of naturalism, faith, politics, education, and society.

Endnotes

1. "Héloïse" is a reference to the 12th century relationship between Abelard and Héloïse. Abelard had been Héloïse's tutor and after the two fell in love and had a child, her uncle had him castrated. Abelard decided they should both devote their lives to God but they wrote passionate letters to each other from their respective monasteries. The letters of Héloïse and Abelard had been published early in the 17th century.